THE COFFEE SELF-TALK DAILY READER #2

MORE BITE-SIZED NUGGETS OF MAGIC TO ADD
TO YOUR MORNING ROUTINE

KRISTEN HELMSTETTER

Green
Butterfly
Press

VI.2

ABOUT THE AUTHOR

In 2018, Kristen Helmstetter sold everything to travel the world with her husband and daughter. She currently lives in a medieval hilltop town in Umbria, Italy.

She writes romance novels under the pen name Brisa Starr.

Listen to *Coffee Self-Talk with Kristen Helmstetter* wherever you listen to podcasts.

You can also find her on Instagram:

instagram.com/coffeeselftalk

OTHER BOOKS BY KRISTEN HELMSTETTER

Coffee Self-Talk: 5 Minutes a Day to Start Living Your Magical Life

The Coffee Self-Talk Daily Reader #1: Bite-Sized Nuggets of Magic to Add to Your Morning Routine

Pillow Self-Talk: 5 Minutes Before Bed to Start Living the Life of Your Dreams

Wine Self-Talk: 15 Minutes to Relax & Tap Into Your Inner Genius

The Coffee Self-Talk Guided Journal: Writing Prompts & Inspiration for Living Your Magical Life

The Coffee Self-Talk Blank Journal (blank with lines)

Coffee Self-Talk for Dudes: 5 Minutes a Day to Start Living Your Legendary Life

Coffee Self-Talk for Teen Girls: 5 Minutes a Day for Confidence, Achievement & Lifelong Happiness

COMING SOON

Money Self-Talk (2022)

CONTENTS

PREFACE

In 2020, I wrote the book, *Coffee Self-Talk*. Since its release, the book has gained a large following of readers, and many of them asked me for more. More ways to augment their morning coffee self-talk ritual, and more ways to add magic to their lives in general.

As it happened, I had a lot more to say!

Because coffee self-talk is a daily ritual, it made sense for me to write a book filled with daily tips and inspiration, which could be read in small bites each day ("nuggets," as I call them), as a supplement to your existing Coffee Self-Talk routine. The result was the *Coffee Self-Talk Daily Reader #1*.

As the "#1" suggests, it was the first in a series of daily readers. The book you now hold in your hands is #2, the second book in that series.

As I stated in #1, my reason for writing these Daily Readers is to help you while you're in the middle of making life changes using Coffee Self-Talk. Think of this as a booster shot. Daily pick-me-ups of happiness and love, ways to add good feelings as you surf the waves of life, and tips for ensuring your success.

This book is not meant to replace your daily Coffee Self-Talk routine. No. This book is for the five-minutes *after* your Coffee Self-Talk ritual. It's for the people who are pumped up, on fire, changing their lives, and wanting to set themselves up for epically successful wins in every way.

Note: If you haven't read *Coffee Self-Talk* yet, I recommend that you read it. While it's not required reading for these Daily Readers, the material it covers is the foundation for your life change. The Daily Readers will still be useful, with all their tips for helping you live a happier and more effective life, but *Coffee Self-Talk* is like the cake, and the Daily Readers are the icing on that cake.

If you are new to Coffee Self-Talk (or if you'd like a quick review), I have included a brief Coffee Self-Talk primer right after the Introduction. Please feel free to skip it if you have recently read *Coffee Self-Talk*.

INTRODUCTION

Dear friend,

It's very exciting to take big steps and bold actions. Like starting a new morning routine doing Coffee Self-Talk. Or making a plan. Or signing up for a class. Or writing the first chapter of a novel. Or taking action toward any goal. Actions like these will light you up! And make you raring to go, champing at the bit to take the next step.

But what if I told you that the *little things* count just as much? In fact, in the long run, tiny actions—the kind you do all day long, often without even thinking about it— these are what really matter. Even more than the occasional big actions.

The Importance of Tiny Acts

It turns out, there are hundreds of tiny, yet mighty things you can do in any given day to keep yourself at peace, elevate your happiness, and draw your dreams and goals to you faster. The tiny size of these strategic micro-actions doesn't matter. They accumulate and compound on one another, gently altering your trajectory, or nudging you back on course, and collectively shaping your destiny.

Some of these tiny actions can have super-sized results, by setting bigger things into motion. Like giving a random compliment to a stranger at a café, and that person becomes a lifelong friend, or perhaps introduces you to an important book, or six months later, mentions a job that you'd be perfect for. You just never know where things will lead.

The Butterfly Effect

It's like the *butterfly effect* from chaos theory, in which a tiny act has huge effects later on. The idea is that a butterfly flapping its wings in Brazil can lead to a hurricane in Texas months later, via the complex interactions of all the air molecules in the atmosphere.

This beautiful metaphor implies an elegant and powerful idea: That even a tiny change in initial conditions—like changing your self-talk, or doing *just one* of the fun activities in this book—can lead to significant, life-changing outcomes at some point in the future.

Every action you take sets in motion a cascading chain reaction of events that lead to a future that has the potential to be vastly different than if you had not taken that initial action. A future starring the new you.

Now imagine, what might happen if you took some of these little, butterfly-wing flappy actions *every day?*

That's what this book is all about. Little ideas to help keep you on your path. And at other times, to help you jump out of your rut onto a completely new path, with potentially huge life changes.

All my very best, and love to you,

Kristen

P.S. For a free, printable PDF with cut-out affirmations and fun reminders to hang on your refrigerator, email me at:

Kristen@KristenHelmstetter.com

Please specify that you'd like the *"Daily Reader #2 Fridge Stuff."* Be sure to include the "#2" so I know which Daily Reader you're referring to.

COFFEE SELF-TALK PRIMER

For Those Who Are New to Coffee Self-Talk

If you have recently read the book, *Coffee Self-Talk,* you can skip this brief section, unless you'd like a quick review.

For those of you who have not read *Coffee Self-Talk*, or who haven't read it in a while, I'll give you a brief overview. I won't go into all the details about positive self-talk, or how life-changing it can be, or why combining it with coffee creates a special kind of daily magic, because covering all that would take a book... one that's already been written. :)

What Is Coffee Self-Talk?

Coffee Self-Talk is a powerful, five-minute program you do every morning while you drink your coffee (or other beverage). It's a special morning ritual with a specific task: reading, thinking—or ideally, speaking out loud—scripts filled with specific words designed to rewire your brain, change your thoughts, your beliefs, your behavior, and your life. It also immediately makes you feel amazing, empowered, and happy.

The scripts you use could be written by you, selected from the scripts provided in the *Coffee Self-Talk* book, or a combination of the two. Many people start with the scripts I provide, and then modify them. People's scripts also change over time, as they progress, or their priorities or life situation changes.

Coffee Self-Talk boosts your confidence and helps you realize your dreams, manifest your goals, and attract the life you've always wanted. It adds more sparkle into your life, more shiny love, more empowerment, and deeper satisfaction. And, importantly, it creates feelings of wholeness, worthiness, and self-love. This last bit is extremely important. Without a sense of self-worth, you're not likely to reach many of your goals because, deep down, you won't feel like you deserve them, and your subconscious mind will sabotage your plans. Coffee Self-Talk is a fun, easy way to fix all that, and get you fired up, shimmering, and sparkling, like you've always deserved.

You are already magical! You always have been! Coffee Self-Talk brings that magic to the surface, where you can wield it to design the life of your dreams.

At the time of this writing, I've recently released a new book, *Pillow Self-Talk*, which you might want to check out. It provides you with a nighttime ritual that's designed to deliver your magical life even faster, by taking advantage of all the amazing things your subconscious mind does while you sleep.

When combined with Coffee Self-Talk in the morning, Pillow Self-Talk creates a powerful process that bookends your day with positive affirmations, self-love, and reflection. Not only does it help you get a great night's sleep, but it also cues things up for an amazing morning, which you then jump right into with your coffee, creating an amazing daily cycle of magical awesomeness!

HOW TO USE THIS DAILY READER

This book is not meant to replace your daily Coffee Self-Talk routine. This book is for the five-minutes *after* your Coffee Self-Talk time.

This book contains 30 "days"—thoughts, ideas, tips, tricks, and activities to amplify the effectiveness of your Coffee Self-Talk ritual.

These are things that have helped me personally to reduce stress and anxiety, increase my resilience, and boost my mood.

Each day is meant to take about five minutes to complete. Some days may take a bit longer. For instance, if you opt to take notes or jot down your thoughts in a notebook or journal, or if the day has an exercise you want to spend a little more time on. It's all up to you.

As this is a "daily" reader, I expect most people will only read one unit per day. You can go through them sequentially, or skip around if you like. If you want to do more than one day at a time, please feel free... though I'd caution against doing too much all at once, as it may dilute the effectiveness. At some point, it's better to let what you've done sink in before moving on to do more.

Some of the days in this book will probably click with you immediately. As you work your way through the days, make a note in your notebook or journal, or simply high-light or bookmark those days that you find most helpful, and then refer back to them in the future, whenever the situation calls for it.

And if some of these techniques *really* resonate with you, you'll want to come back to them regularly. When you do this, they'll become ingrained in you, as part of your default go-to response when something happens in life that you need help navigating with grace. So, although the magic nuggets are bite-sized, and spaced out as one per day, don't be surprised if you find yourself coming back to a certain handful of them that you love.

The Exercises

Some of the days in this book contain exercises. Some-thing small and uplifting, and they'll usually only take a few minutes to complete, unless you want to expand upon them. I recommend that you do the exercises. Not only to get the most of out of this book, but also to have fun!

On some days, I may ask you to pull up your smart phone's calendar, or your to-do list, or your notebook or journal, if you're using one. And some of the exercises will involve sticky notes (or scraps of paper and tape... whatever you have). On "sticky note days," if time permits, you might want to get creative with your color pens, and possibly stickers, for extra flair. I decorate mine elaborately. Seriously, I go nuts.

All right. Let's get started.

DAY 1: HOW CAN I LOVE MYSELF MORE TODAY?

"You yourself, as much as anybody in the entire universe, deserve your love and affection."

— THE BUDDHA

Self-love should be easy for people, but sometimes they think of self-love as doing big things, like taking a day (or week) off, or standing up for your personal time when you feel guilty for taking it, or taking time to exercise or meditate every day. And then they never do it, because it's too big. Too daunting.

Those are all significant acts of self-love, but self-love comes in all sizes. As with so many large, seemingly insurmountable tasks, it's often best to break them down into small parts, and then focus your energy on just one, easy piece. And then, after starting with small, micro-acts of self-love, the momentum builds. Which makes it easier to do more micro-acts of self-love, and these collectively set you up for a big act of self-love, like a volleyball player setting up the ball for a teammate to spike. Boom!

The way to think of micro-acts of self-love is with one simple question:

How can I love myself more today?

When you ask yourself this, the sky will open up and sprinkle down all kinds of sparkly stars of self-love you can play with, that don't take much effort, and they don't take much time, but their effects can be huge.

Here is just a sample of all the ways I answer the question, *Kristen, how can I love myself more today?*

- *I can smile right now.*
- *I can stand up and stretch.*
- *I can pee when I actually need to and not hold it as I try to cram in more work.*
- *I can have an extra cup of green tea.*
- *I can rub lotion into my hands.*
- *I can get into bed ten minutes earlier with a book.*
- *I can call my friend.*
- *I can watch my favorite show on Netflix.*
- *I can play a game of solitaire.*
- *I can play a game of UNO with my daughter.*
- *I can go for a five-minute walk.*
- *I can pat myself on the back, just because I'm worthy.*
- *I can order takeout and not cook tonight.*
- *I can ask my husband to empty the dishwasher.*
- *I can paint my nails.*

- *I can eat white chocolate with caramel inside.*
- *I can look in the mirror and say, "I love you."*

See how easy these are? No guilt. No drama. No tradeoffs. Just easy little sparklets of self-love, any time you want.

Your Turn to Play!

Get out your notebook, or journal, or a piece of paper, and write at the top of a blank page, *How can I love myself more today?*

Think of five things you can do and write them down. Then, carry this list around with you today, in your pocket or purse, or copy the list onto a slip of paper if you can't carry your notebook/journal around. Read it multiple times throughout the day, and do at least one of the items you listed.

Also, add a weekly reminder on your calendar for a *Self-Love Micro-Act Day* where you read this list and do something on it.

You deserve to live the life of your dreams!

Today's affirmation:

I'm falling in love with myself, and it's the greatest love affair ever!

DAY 2: ABUNDANCE: THE KNOWN AND UNKNOWN

"Happiness, like unhappiness, is a proactive choice."

— STEPHEN R. COVEY

Abundance will come to you from sources both known *and* unknown. That is, some of them will surprise you.

Goals are great. They're a powerful tool. They give you direction and motivation, encouraging you to take action. They also focus your energies. But sometimes, this focus limits your ability to see more broadly. As you work toward some specific result, it's possible to miss what else is going on, or unexpected opportunities.

For instance, if you seek financial abundance, it's good to work toward financial goals, but you also want to be open to abundance that comes from both known *and unknown* sources. For example, your job might bring a regular, known income, but you might receive income in other ways that you hadn't expected.

Unknown sources. And sometimes in forms other than money.

When we moved to Italy, we had income from a variety of sources... books, my blog, my husband's consulting work, and so on. These were expected. What was unexpected, was that our wonderful landlord would bring us a basket of fresh vegetables from his garden every day... a staggering bounty of color, with heirloom varieties I'd never seen before. And bottles of olive oil from his orchard. Or a loaf of fresh-baked bread!

To a foodie like me, these were riches beyond compare. I could never put a dollar value on it, but the important thing is to recognize wealth and abundance in all of its wild, wooly, and wonderful forms.

You just never know what the universe is going to toss your way.

Always be ready to catch it.

This can happen with love, too. When you're manifesting more love in your life, be very aware that it can come in all forms. Expect the unexpected! And recognize it when it shows up!

Yes, the expected forms of love come from family and romantic partners. But the world is so full of unexpected forms of love, too. And they matter! Kindnesses from strangers, coworkers... even animals. OMG, animals... they have so much love to give, I sometimes wonder if they would spend their manifesting-bucks on just finding one person who's willing to receive all they have to give.

All of these are forms of love, whether expected or unexpected.

The lesson is to remember that, when you are manifesting your dreams, your life is made more magical when you see how often you draw to you from both kinds of sources, the known and the unknown. It's times like these that your life feels extra sparkly!

In my experience, the unexpected forms are the best kind. Which kinda makes all of your goals, striving, and hard work take a back seat to the mystery of the universe and its amazing gifts. Let that sink in for a minute. It's important to plan, work, expend effort, and go for it... but realize that, not only is there more out there... it's very possible that the "more" actually is MORE.

For this reason, I have the following line in my Coffee Self-Talk:

I get abundance from known and unknown sources. My hands and arms are open to it all. Abundance rains down from everywhere to me.

Always remember, you are dancing with the universe, but it all starts with YOU. You are the one making it happen by attracting it with your high energy, your elevated emotions, your beautiful attitude.

Your Turn to Play!

Pay attention today (and every day), and be on the lookout for any type of abundance that comes your way from an unexpected source.

Note it in your notebook or journal, if you have one. These notes will seem similar to general statements of gratitude, with one important difference: *They are new.*

When you receive something new that's worthy of your gratitude—assuming you're being mindful and noticing when good things happen—be sure to call them out. Write them down. Keep track. These become assets on your cosmic balance sheet, in which abundance flows in all kinds of forms. And then give thanks, and say out loud, "Yes! More of this, please!"

You are dazzling.

Today's affirmation:

I stand up, open my palms to the world, ready to receive my dreams.

DAY 3: MAGICAL LIFE MINUTE

"Control of consciousness determines the quality of life."

— MIHALY CSIKSZENTMIHALYI

In the book, *Coffee Self-Talk*, I share with you something I do called my *Millionaire Minute*. For today's exercise, I've adapted that passage from the book, and I'm calling it your *Magical Life Minute*, because not everybody is seeking financial abundance.

Or you could call it your *Magical Healing Minute* if you're seeking health, or your *Magical Longevity Minute* if you're dreaming about being alive to see hotels on the moon. Or your *Magical Love Minute*, if you're drawing a future to you filled with love, romance, and excitement with a wonderful, significant other. Pick something you're working on manifesting.

What Is the Magical Life Minute?

The *Magical Life Minute* is a potent technique I use to create an empowered mental and emotional state, any time I want.

Here's how it works. I've set an alarm on my cell phone to go off several times during the day. When the alarm goes off, it plays a specific piece of music that I've anchored, and it serves to trigger—in my case—my *Happy Sexy Millionaire* state... that's what I've named the dream life I'm drawing to me. It comprises the thoughts, feelings, visualizations, and general mindset I've associated with manifesting my Happy Sexy Millionaire self.

When the alarm goes off, I stop whatever I'm doing, close my eyes, and focus on these thoughts and feelings related to becoming a Happy Sexy Millionaire. For me, that means I'm instantly *feeling* my Happy Sexy Millionaire life. I'm experiencing it as if it's real, in that moment. I sense shimmeriness and golden light all around me, I'm excited, and I'm overflowing with confidence. In that moment, I'm *happy, sexy, and rich!*

What does this do? Well, I've anchored that particular song to feeling outstanding, because I always listen to it while I read my Coffee Self-Talk. I've done it every day, for months and months... and that piece of music has become deeply ingrained in my neurons, and it's extremely effective at triggering the mental state I've anchored it to.

When the alarm goes off, I'm reminded of my powerful Coffee Self-Talk that makes me feel like a million bucks. It reminds me I'm manifesting that life every day. Not just with positive thoughts, but with every action I take, and all the effort, and love, and passion, and commitment I put into my work. This reminder instantly sets my brain to maximum level of feeling good and uplifted. It taps me into the life I'm manifesting.

Sometimes, when the alarm goes off, I imagine a gold box being delivered to my front door, decked out with a sparkling red bow, and the box is filled with a million dollars. It's not that I necessarily expect my fortune to actually arrive like that (but, hey, who knows, right?). Rather, it's a picture in my head that symbolizes just how easy it is to manifest what I want. It's a mental hack really, tricking the brain into getting the subconscious bits on board, so everybody's pulling in the same direction. Meaning all of my actions are aligned with my goals, and I'm not conflicted, distracted, or self-sabotaging.

It's also really fun to visualize this. It really works... it changes my mood and mindset *instantly*.

It's an amazing state of mind, and I try to live in it all day long, but sometimes, the mundane details of existence, like doing laundry, paying bills, or buying groceries cause me to momentarily forget about my epic, shiny, golden mission.

And then, suddenly, *My Millionaire Minute* alarm goes off!

And... BAM!

When I hear the opening notes of the music, I'm instantly transported into that mental space where all the magic happens. After about 20-60 seconds, I stop the music and resume whatever I was doing, except now with a super-charged sense of purpose and a refreshed outlook.

And this happens five times a day!

I've set the alarm on my iPhone to go off at 10:00 AM, 12:00 PM, 2:00 PM, 4:00 PM, and 6:00 PM. At those times, my phone is programmed to the electronic ambient song, *Liquid Flow,* by Dreaming Cooper. It's kind of futuristic and instantly resets my brain from whatever I was doing, to being 100% focused on manifestation. It's amazing.

The alarms repeat every day.

Your Turn to Play!

Create your own *Magical Life Minute,* (that is, if you haven't done it already, from reading about it in *Coffee Self-Talk*). If you're already doing Coffee Self-Talk each day, then you already have some experience with thinking about and feeling the life you're dreaming of. If you haven't, spend some time trying to imagine how you would feel, right now, if your dream life had already manifested, and you were living it every day. The more details you imagine, the better.

Next, find a song that you'd like to anchor to these thoughts and feelings. It should be a song that resonates with you in the first few seconds, something that immediately grabs your attention. It should also be a song that isn't already strongly anchored to something else, like senior year in high school, or a road trip, etc.

And finally, on your phone, set an alarm for that song, set to go off 4 to 6 times a day. Every time this song goes off, if it's safe to do so, close your eyes, take a deep breath, and take a moment to draw your future to you with elevated thoughts and feelings, thinking and feeling it, as you listen, visualizing the details of living in your dream life... almost like you're in a movie of that reality.

After doing this several times a day, every day, for maybe a couple of weeks, you'll start anchoring the song to these thoughts, feelings, and visions. And then, every time your Magical Life Minute alarm goes off, you'll be instantly transported in your heart and mind to this wonderful, magical place you're creating.

You are unstoppable!

~

Today's affirmation:

I love taking time for myself, because I am worthy.

DAY 4: INSTANT ENERGY

"Learn to get excited like a child. There is nothing that has more magic than childish excitement."

— JIM ROHN

If you find yourself tired all the time, you might not be getting enough sleep. And if you're not getting enough sleep, well, there are plenty of books about the importance of sleep, so I won't address that here. (Short version: Sleep is *really* important for your mental and physical health.)

But that's not the kind of tiredness I'm talking about.

I'm talking about the listless, droopy, low-energy state that so many people exhibit when they lack purpose or excitement in their lives.

Is this you?

If not, that's great! If it is, then read on...

When you don't have anything in your life that makes you excited to bounce out of bed, it's like the mind and body are pretending they're still in bed... all day long! Assuming there are no underlying health issues, if you don't have enough energy, could it be that you don't have enough stuff you're excited about?

This is a fascinating idea when you think about it. The brain seeks to optimize. This includes conserving energy when it's not needed. When you don't have stuff to be excited about, it makes sense that your brain would dial down your energy level, making you feel tired. And worse, adding darkness, blah, and boredom to a life that was already a bit dark, blah, and boring.

How can you break this vicious cycle?

Here's a thought experiment. Imagine you're sprawled out on your couch with droopy eyes, drool coming out of your mouth, eating a bag of chips, watching some random show because you have nothing exciting going on.

Suddenly, your doorbell rings.

You shuffle to the door with your head down, shoulders hunched. You answer the door, and someone presents you with an envelope with a $1000 in cash. It's totally legit.

How would you feel? Would you be excited? Would you have a surge in energy? Of course you would!

Or what if your spouse came home and said, "Honey, let's go away for the weekend!" And you were just lying on the couch, tired, frumpy. You would probably jump up, ready to research places to go. You would have a surge in energy.

Sometimes I have been lying on the couch, thinking I might take a nap, and my husband will look up from his computer and say something like, "Someone just ordered twenty books to donate to women's shelters." I suddenly want to jump up and dance! Or maybe he says, "I've got a new business idea," and the excitement sends a ripple of energy through me.

Think about how profound this is. My physical state changed instantly, not because I just suddenly got miracle sleep, or took a stimulant, but because a switch flipped in my head! That's how powerful your thoughts are. They CAN change your reality. In this example, all it took was receiving some new piece of information that jazzed me up.

But you don't need to wait for a knock at the door, or for your partner to suggest doing something fun. All that is required is that YOU make a decision.

A decision to do *something that excites you.*

So, the next time you're feeling listless and low-energy, look around at your life and the things going on in a typical day. Maybe you just need something to be excited about. It could be a new hobby—tennis, quilting, cooking, building an aquarium, flying a drone... anything. Or you could think of a way to make extra income—selling stuff on eBay, Etsy... there are hundreds of low-cost ways to get started. Or you could take a vacation, or you could get lost in a new book. You could volunteer somewhere and make another person's life better. Or volunteer at an animal shelter. You could go back to school, or take classes online, or learn some cool skill from watching YouTube videos. You could go after something you've always wanted to do.

I don't know about you, but to me, *all* of these sound better than drooling on the couch!

When you realize there are things that 1) have the power to make you jump up off the couch, and 2) you have the power to summon this energy simply by *making a decision*... your whole world opens up to one of possibilities.

It doesn't matter if there's nobody knocking on your door, offering you a bag full of gold. You have that bag of gold inside of yourself. All you have to do is open it, and reach inside.

Your Turn to Play!

Think about things that get you excited and juiced. Make a list of twenty items. Yes, *twenty!* Write them down.

Do you get excited by the idea of taking a fun, spontaneous road trip? Trying a new restaurant? Helping someone out? Planning a party? Starting a new hobby? Rejuvenating your interest in an old hobby? Is it starting a new book series? Maybe you've always wanted to learn how to dance salsa.

Make your list! And then take action on one of the items. It can be a tiny action, but do *something*.

You are fab, baby. You light up the room!

Today's affirmation:

I am full of power. Here and now.

DAY 5: SMILE DAY

"I've got nothing to do today but smile."

— SIMON AND GARFUNKEL

Here is some amazing science on smiling and why we're going to make it your focus today.

When you're happy, you smile. (You knew that.) But did you know that it works in reverse? That when you smile, it can also make you happy? Yes, it can!

How cool is this? Studies show that smiling, even if you're forcing or faking the smile, can actually make you happier! It reduces stress and makes you feel happier by tricking your brain. When you force a smile, you contract muscles in your face that trigger a release of happiness neurotransmitters in your brain, which in turn, make you smile, creating a *happiness feedback loop.*

Smiling is also contagious for those around you. According to neuroscientist Marco Iacoboni,

> "When I see you smiling, my mirror neurons for smiling fire up, too, initiating a cascade of neural activity that evokes the feeling we typically associate with a smile. I don't need to make any inference on what you are feeling, I experience immediately and effortlessly a milder form of what you are experiencing."

Why smile as often as possible? Because smiling is linked with happier lives, happier marriages, and longer life. You know by now that feeling elevated emotions is important, a critical part of the manifestation recipe. But I'll say it again because repetition is powerful: When you feel elevated emotions like happiness, love, gratitude, it helps you manifest your magical life faster.

With that in mind, you can use this smile science as a sort of happiness hack. Knowing that you can smile, and that it'll elevate your emotions, means you now have a great trick up your sleeve for managing how you feel at any given time, such as if you're feeling down, or simply doing something less than inspiring, such as taxes, or cleaning the toilet. Just keep on smiling!

But let's take this clever trick one step further. The next time you feel any kind of anxiety, or frustration, or impatience, or stress... if you drop something and it breaks, or if you have an argument with your partner or a coworker, or you just wake up feeling blue, or have doubts about life or anything... just smile. *Smile! Smile! Smile!*

It might feel weird at first, or unnatural. I mean, it will, actually. But that's ok—it's not quite natural... you're hacking your brain. Just keep smiling anyway.

You might feel goofy. That's ok. In fact, that's good. Goofiness is 75% of the way to happiness. Just keep going.

Your Turn to Play!

Want to try it now?

It's easy. Plaster a big, beautiful or goofy, playful grin on your face, and keep it there for at least thirty seconds. Set a timer to see how long you can go, and when you get to thirty seconds, notice how you feel. Do you feel wonderfully ticklish inside, like little champagne bubbles are coursing through your veins?

Do this as often as you can during the day. Get comfortable with it. *It's magical.*

You're a glowing ray of sunshine.

~

Today's affirmation:

I love smiling. It brightens my life.

DAY 6: SYNERGY DAY

"And hand in hand, on the edge of the sand,

They danced by the light of the moon."

— EDWARD LEAR, THE OWL AND THE PUSSYCAT

Today is about *synergy*, which is when two things combine in a way that's more than when the two things stand alone.

We're going to talk about sharing the *new you* you're becoming, with someone else. This sharing could simply mean telling someone what you're up to. Sharing with them how you're drawing your dreams to you. Or you could share a goal of yours, letting the person know what you're working toward.

Why? Because when somebody else knows your goal, it creates a level of accountability. Research has shown that most people will do more to keep a promise to others than a promise to themselves. Use this to your advantage!

But even more incredible is that when you share what you're doing, you get that person's buy-in, and you benefit from any energy or excitement they have for your plans, which propels you more.

Of course, you'll want to carefully choose the person (or people) you tell. If they aren't the type to be supportive of your dreams, or if they just won't "get it," then they're not the ones to share this personal information with. But if they are the right kind of person, then sharing can be very fun! (If there's nobody in your life that will understand, then tell the wonderful people at the Coffee Self-Talk Facebook group! — Facebook.com/groups/coffeeselftalk)

I have a core group of friends who love hearing what I'm up to. Every time I share a new goal with them, or celebrate a victory, they share in my energy and excitement. It also inspires them! And this increases the energy I can tap into for manifesting my own magical life. And I provide the same excitement and support for their goals and dreams.

Synergy is power! We are all stronger when we bond together.

Your Turn to Play!

Share what you're doing with somebody, be it a friend, family member, or coworker. Heck, it can be a complete stranger in the grocery store checkout line. What you share can be something as simple as, *I'm on a new journey, and I'm excited about it!* If they ask questions, then load 'em up with the details.

Or you could share about a specific goal you have, whether that's working on loving yourself more, or making a million bucks, or learning to scuba dive. A dear friend of mine recently shared with me her goal to become a helicopter pilot, and it still makes me vicariously excited every time I think about it! I'll be absolutely thrilled for her when she gets her license! See how we both benefit from this sharing?

If you don't have someone you feel comfortable sharing this amazing stuff with, you can always email me!

Kristen@KristenHelmstetter.com

I'd love to hear from you. We can all help each other!

You are awesome.

~

Today's affirmation:

I love being generous with myself, and I love being generous with others. We are all one.

DAY 7: REJOICE IN... WHAT?

"Who is the happiest man? He who is alive to the merit of others, and can rejoice in their enjoyment as if it were his own."

— JOHANN WOLFGANG VON GOETHE

Yesterday, I talked about sharing your goals with someone else. Today is nearly the opposite. It might feel a little strange at first, but the more you do it, the more natural it will feel. Like... this is the way the world was meant to be.

I'm talking about the idea of celebrating other people's triumphs. Appreciating their wins. You can *"rejoice in the success of others,"* like author Louise Hay says, or like Goethe said in the opening quote, two centuries ago. That word—*rejoice*—seems so antiquated, right? But it *packs a punch!*

Maybe you already do this. If so, that's great, and maybe do it *even more!* If you don't, don't worry. It's human nature to run any news through the "how is this relevant to me?" filter. And that's your ego asking the question. And it's not necessarily bad.

But where things go south is when we hear good news about others, and it makes us feel bad. Don't give in to this! That's the ego trying to measure your worth by comparing yourself to others. But you must always keep in mind… you are *already worthy!* You have nothing to prove! Not to you, and not to anybody else.

And when you feel worthy, the comparisons magically just stop.

Why? Because when you're worthy, your heart is full of love. It *overflows* with love. It's got so much love, that you not only love yourself, but you also love everyone else. And because you love others, genuinely, deep down, you feel nothing but happiness when good things happen to them.

Rejoicing in the success of others is simply the emotion of compassion, but applied to others' good news instead of bad.

When other people succeed, you want to *dance for their success*, not scrunch your mouth down in a jealous frown. Whether it's friends, or family, or coworkers, do a cheer every time they win. Did your neighbor just get a new job? Did a friend just post pics of their tropical vacation on Instagram, and you wish you could take a trip, too? Did a coworker just write a novel, and you secretly always wanted to write one? Celebrate with them!

When you jump for joy at another's accomplishment, it's a significant way to elevate your mindset *and your heart*.

Why is this important? Because it improves your state. Because it's a good thing to do. Because it helps you more than you might think.

You see—again, it's totally natural—for many people, they feel a twinge of jealousy when someone else is succeeding. Or they feel a sense of lack, or like they're being left behind. Or, heck, sometimes it's full-blown, green-eyed envy. And don't get me started on how we can sometimes feel when it's someone succeeding that you don't super-duper love, right? Or—*gasp*—someone that you've always seen as a "competitor."

But jealousy and envy aren't elevated emotions! No! No! They never will be. And they'll slam on the brakes to living your magical life, giving you emotional whiplash. They put you in the slowpoke lane to manifesting your own dreams. So let's unpack this a bit...

Why is it natural to feel envy? Why don't we just naturally dance for other people's success all the time?

It comes down to that gnarly feeling of scarcity. The idea that, because someone else got something, it means there's not enough for you. But here's the thing. You want to get rid of that *lack* mentality entirely. Shush that scarcity mindset. Because the truth is that there is *plenty to go around*. Always! There are opportunities everywhere. And it is not fun to be jealous. It friggin' sucks.

But when you embrace the mindset that there is *plenty for everybody*, that there's tons of love to be had, and tons of money to attract, and tons of happiness available to all, then you'll grow your spirit in a *very* special way: It tells your subconscious that *these things are abundant*, and that you can have them, too.

Your emotional response might be instantaneous. In a mind-boggling, galactic-love-spreading way. Your nerves are soothed. Your anxiety chills the f*ck out. And all kinds of wonderful shimmers around you.

Try these words on for size. Imagine someone you know just told you something they were happy about, and you say to yourself (and say it like you *really* mean it),

I celebrate that woman's success.

I dance a happy dance for that dude's win.

I love that they're making so much money.

I'm so happy she found the love of her life.

It's empowering. It makes you a bigger person. A badass. And even though it felt strange the first time I uttered words like this, I was blown away when I let the words cross my lips. *"I rejoice in her success. I celebrate her accomplishment! Yes!"*

It felt... *unified.*

Why unified? Because *we are all one*. When you celebrate another's win, it spreads love. This creates a richness in your heart. A sense of security. And, funny thing, you might even feel more *mature* when you adopt this mindset... at least, I did, lol!

Here's the bottom line:

When you embrace this attitude, you attract more fortune to yourself.

Oh yeah, baby. That's how it works. It feels good, and it brings good.

What a difference to celebrate everybody else's wins.

Your Turn to Play!

Make it a point to naturally feel happy and excited for others' successes.

If you currently know of somebody—perhaps a friend, coworker, or a family member—who has experienced success that made you feel envious, even if only in a playful way, then take a moment to close your eyes and send that person love, congratulations, and a mental high-five. The idea is to feel genuine pleasure in knowing that it's making *them happy*. (My husband's variant of this is to mentally raise his glass to the person and say, *Well done, you deserve it.*)

Notice how you feel when you do this. If you find it difficult, then keep doing it longer. If it makes you feel good... this is what it feels like to rejoice in the success of others.

When you extend love in this way, you automatically love yourself a little bit more in that moment, and you start to reframe success as an abundant resource, which you yourself are worthy of having. *Which is a great feeling to have!*

If you feel no envy toward anybody, that's terrific! If you don't have a situation right now for practicing this, consider adding a few related lines to your Coffee Self-Talk, such as:

I rejoice in the massive success of others!

I dance for another's win!

I'm so happy when others kick ass!

I also recommend you write an affirmation of self-talk like this on a sticky note and stick it on your bathroom mirror, or on your desk. Every time you see it, take a moment to read it and feel peace inside yourself when others are succeeding. Let it inspire you, and notice how your attitude about *abundance for yourself* improves over time.

You are an incredible, fun, and interesting person.

Today's affirmation:

I wake up every morning with warmth in my heart for the world.

DAY 8: ASKING FOR HELP

"We all live with the objective of being happy; our lives are all different and yet the same."

— ANNE FRANK

Do you have trouble asking for help? Maybe even for the smallest thing, like asking your husband or partner to take out the trash?

I hear from a lot of women who have a hard time asking for help. They feel like they need to be supermom, or that they're less of a badass because they asked for help with household chores. Perhaps this attitude comes from the 1950s, when something shifted. Women started going to work, but they never offloaded the tasks at home. And they took on this *"I must do everything on my own to succeed"* mentality to work, and some have a hard time asking for help in the workplace.

I understand this mentality. I used to have it myself. It started when I had my daughter. I erroneously felt that, because my husband was the main breadwinner at the time (I was writing a blog and making some money, but he brought in the bulk of our income), everything involving the baby was my responsibility—changing diapers, feeding her, doing laundry, and so on.

The thought of asking my husband to wake up in the middle of the night to take care of her was out of the question. I felt way too guilty. Even though I was chronically sleep deprived.

What a crappy way to live. And a brilliant way to build up resentment between people. The crazy thing is, my husband was happy to help. It was I who was unwilling to ask, or to even just let him know I needed it.

One day, that all changed when I asked him to help with something involving our baby daughter. I'd finally had enough. My hair was greasy, I'd worn the same clothes for days, and I hadn't put on makeup in a week.

"Sure," he said. I was a bit shocked that he was so quick to help. I was even mildly suspicious, but my exhaustion took over, and I told him what I needed him to do.

Why hadn't I asked him for help earlier? Because I didn't feel worthy. I felt the burden was mine alone. As a mother.

This is a common sentiment. Some people don't ask for help because they don't feel worthy of receiving it.

Or they don't ask for help because they think the other person won't do as good a job. I was so guilty of this! I wouldn't even let my husband do the food shopping for fear that he wouldn't pick out the best cucumbers or broccoli. He literally offered, multiple times, and I said no.

Both of these things—feeling unworthy or feeling like you're the only one who can do the job correctly—breed negative emotions. And negative emotions are boulders on the path between you and living your most epic life.

One day, I realized this. "Duh, Kristen. Just ask for help."

Since then, it's been ten years of letting my husband know my needs. All the time. I now don't think twice before asking. *"Hey, babe, I need your help"* or *"Hey, handsome, rugged husband, please do this."*

And? He easily and quickly gets up to do it. Well, ok, sometimes his more relaxed time frame doesn't match mine, but it's usually not his fault. It's my own impatience. But impatience is a topic for another day. (This reminds me of the old joke, *"If I say I'll do something, I'll do it. You don't need to nag me every six months."*)

This doesn't just apply to spouses. I had to learn to ask my daughter for help, once she was old enough. And my mom. And friends.

I even had to overcome my natural resistance to asking for help when it came to asking readers to leave reviews for my books on Amazon. Like it or not, it's simply part of the job of being an author in the modern online world. The funny thing is, my resistance was unnecessary. Readers usually wrote back saying they'd be happy to help. Sometimes their replies even had multiple exclamation points and heart emojis.

Here's the thing: *Most people want to help.*

Think about it... don't you take minor pleasure in helping a stranger with directions? Or telling someone who is about to walk away without noticing that she has left her purse behind? Most people are good like this. It's rare to find somebody who doesn't want to help, especially if you ask them. It might only take one or two times asking for help to make you realize how simple it is.

The purpose of today's activity is to open yourself to the idea of asking for help, and accepting when it's offered, if the situation warrants.

When you do, something beautiful happens. You'll discover that moving through the world, open to help, asking for assistance, gets easier and easier with practice.

It'll touch you how many people willingly and happily want to help, in all kinds of ways. And you'll connect more deeply with people by asking for, and accepting, their help.

Benjamin Franklin once won over a political adversary by asking him if he could borrow one of the books from the man's personal library. The man was taken aback, but then obliged, and loaned Franklin the book. And forever after that, the man treated Franklin as a friend.

When you ask someone for help, it forges new bonds and strengthens existing ones. This creates elevated emotions... you know, the *feelings we love for attracting our dreams!*

When you ask for help at home, whether from a child, or a spouse, or a sibling, and they do it, notice the sense of respect that you feel when they do it, a subtle feeling of honor that they were willing to help you. The synergy that comes from cooperation makes the energy in the whole house become brighter.

Finally, when you open yourself to receiving help, you are showing the universe that you're worthy and open to receiving its gifts. It helps reinforce your attitudes about abundance, making you more willing to help others, and benefiting from the joy that brings.

Your Turn to Play!

Write the following on three sticky notes:

I am open to receiving help.

Then add it once to your phone (or to-do list/calendar/notebook/etc.).

Place your sticky notes someplace where you'll see them.

This is the only thing you need to do today. But if you're ready to take it to the next level, go out into the world and find just one way that you can ask for help, as practice, to become more comfortable doing it.

Soon, and for the rest of life, you'll be open to receiving help from others.

You are amazing.

∾

Today's affirmation:

It's easy asking for help. I am open to receiving it.

DAY 9: FIVE SENSES IN FIVE MINUTES

"The power of finding beauty in the humblest things makes home happy and life lovely."

— LOUISA MAY ALCOTT

Being mindful and fully present in the moment is a fantastic way to reduce anxiety and stress. This is because, when you are existing in the moment, you are not dwelling about the past or worrying about the future. Being mindful is powerful, and it can help ease anxiety and depression immediately. And if you do it regularly enough, in the long run, it can hardwire your brain to be more calm in general, able to bob and dance with life's ups and downs, like a daisy in the breeze.

Using your senses is a simple way to tap into mindfulness, and I'll explain how to do it in a moment. When you do this, if you're uptight about something, it'll help you relax those survival emotions, helping you shift into elevated emotions for living a magical life.

Practicing mindfulness like you'll do in today's exercise also helps to increase focus, improve sleep, and boost your energy because, when you're being mindful and fully present for a few minutes, your brain and body get a rest from everything else that's going on in your life.

Your Turn to Play!

Spend the next five minutes paying attention to each of your senses, for one minute each. No opinions, no mental rabbit holes to go down. Just a pure, delicious, perfectly divine, gluttonous sensory experience.

Seeing

Set a timer for one minute, and look around, noticing anything and everything within your field of vision. Look at your hands, the wall, the ceiling, the table, the sky, the appliances or furniture in the room, your clothes, or feet, or hair... One minute, only looking.

Hearing

Set a timer for one minute, and close your eyes to help you focus on only listening. Can you hear the refrigerator humming? Or the central heat or air conditioning? Dogs barking? Cars driving by? Birds chirping? Your neighbor's leaf blower? If you'd like, you can use an app on your phone that plays a constant sound like white noise, or waves, or crystal bowl chimes. One minute, only listening.

Tasting

Set a timer for one minute, and have something to eat or drink. For a more effective experience, keep your eyes closed. You can even wear earplugs, to increase the tasting sensory experience. If you're not hungry or thirsty right now, then perhaps just get a glass of water or an ice cube. And for the minute, take sips and taste it. This one is easier to do with something with a strong flavor, but even with plain water, if you focus on it, you'll find throughout the minute that it does have a taste. One minute, only tasting.

Touching

Set a timer for one minute and focus on feeling physical objects. You can get up and move around for this. You can touch your skin, your clothing, your coffee mug, the couch or chair, the floor under your feet, a doorknob, water running over your hands—anything you want to feel–just focus on the texture of the item. You could also do this sitting down, eyes closed, ears plugged, holding something in your hand, and letting yourself experience it with minimal other senses involved. One minute, only touching.

Smelling

This one can be a little tricky, but do your best. If you're eating food or drinking something, then you can focus on smelling just that. You can breathe into your hand and smell your breath. (I'm serious.) You can get a bunch of spices from your pantry and open them up and smell them. You can smell flowers if you have any nearby. One minute, smelling only.

When you're done with all five senses, take a moment and notice where you are, emotionally speaking. Do you feel more grounded in the present moment?

This is something you can do any time, any place. You're in control.

You are worthy, wonderful, and lovely.

Today's affirmation:

I am full of kindness. I see it, hear it, say it, feel it all day long.

DAY 10: SHUSHING SHOULDS

"The happiness of your life depends upon the quality of your thoughts."

— Marcus Aurelius

Some time ago, I tossed the word "should" from my vocabulary. It felt superb to do it.

It was Anita Moorjani who made me see the word differently. When she advised against using the word, I thought, *Huh... ok, I'll try it.* But I wasn't entirely convinced.

However, the first time I caught myself saying it, I remembered to hit the mental *delete* key. Hm... I felt quite different. In that instant, I felt better.

I've since tossed "should" from my vocabulary, and I never looked back. It seemed so simple when Anita talked about it. Funny, too, because it never dawned on me how damaging the word "should" could be, until I stopped saying it.

Think about it.

Think of all the times you use the word *should*, and then think about how you feel when you say it. It's a word that sneaks in there and screws up your self-talk, but no one really notices because it's so common.

- I should work out more.
- I should eat less sugar.
- I should get to bed earlier.
- I should drink less alcohol.
- I should call my mom more often.
- I should save more money.
- I should work more.
- I should stop eating so much chocolate.
- I should, I should, I should.

These statements are *not* empowering.

And they're not creating elevated emotions. Remember, to manifest your dreams, you want to feel elevated as often as possible. Cutting out *should* is low-hanging fruit when it comes to pursuing your magical life.

Now, I'm not talking about harmless instances of the word, like, *"Hey honey, we should stop by the store on the way home."* But since I've eliminated the word from my vocabulary, as a matter of habit, now I'd say something like, *"Hey honey, let's stop by the store on the way home."*

Notice how it feels more intentional this way? More like we're in charge? "Should" subtly suggests that some external will is being imposed upon us.

When you give yourself permission to never use the word *should* again, your life might shift noticeably. Your mood may lighten a bit. You may also feel like a weight has been lifted from your shoulders.

Affirmation guru Louise Hay said,

> "Should is one of the most damaging words in our language. Every time we use should, we are, in effect, saying 'wrong.' Either we are wrong, or we were wrong, or we are going to be wrong. I don't think we need more wrongs in our life."

Why Shushing Your Shoulds Works

Take this example:

> "I should work out today."

This can leave you feeling crummy and guilty. But replacing *should* with a better word can make you feel better, because the guilt is gone. Guilt is not an elevated emotion. In this way, you can see how *shushing your shoulds* is a subtle, yet effective little verbal trick.

The word *should* is linked to *needs*. And when we have needs, it's easy to tumble down a rabbit hole thinking about everything that's lacking in your life. And thinking about lack too often creates negative emotions, survival emotions. And survival emotions are not elevated emotions. Saying *should* risks bringing your energy down. Now, this might not happen every time, but it's enough that changing your language to remove some *shoulds* might be beneficial.

Whenever I catch myself about to say it, and I let it go, I feel a sense of relief.

Replacing Should with Could

Every time you catch yourself using the word *should,* try replacing it with *could,* and watch how your experience changes. Watch how it magically morphs into an experience of empowerment, of choice, of freedom. *Of possibilities!*

Here are the statements from above, but with *should* replaced by *could:*

- I could work out more.
- I could eat less sugar.
- I could get to bed earlier.
- I could drink less alcohol.
- I could call my mom more often.
- I could save more money.
- I could work more.
- I could stop eating so much chocolate.
- I could, I could, I could.

See the power? The new choice you've given yourself?

Note: Simply ditching *should* from your vocabulary is a great place to start and bring more happiness into your life. Occasionally, you can throw in a *could* to spark motivation, but it's not necessary every time.

You possess unlimited possibilities.

∾

Today's affirmation:

Everything is possible. I open my eyes to the sky. I fill my heart with love, and I'm on my way. Here I come!

DAY 11: I LOVE MYSELF ANYWAY

> "It was only a sunny smile, and little it cost in the giving, but like morning light it scattered the night and made the day worth living."

> — F. Scott Fitzgerald

I love myself anyway.

No matter what is going on in your life, no matter what you'd like to change... today, you love yourself anyway.

For example, *"I love myself, even though I'm in debt."*

Or, *"I want to lose weight, but I love myself anyway."*

Or, *"Even though I want a better job, I love myself anyway."*

Today, I want you to love yourself *anyway.*

That means you love yourself, no matter what. Unconditionally.

I want you to look at your body and love it, no matter what. I want you to look at your bank account, and if it's lower than you want, you love it anyway. In fact, you can even think about that low or empty bank account (or the debt you might have, or the extra fat around your waist that you'd like to lose), and you can love it anyway, too!

That's what I did one day toward my debt. That's what I wanted to change. Getting out of debt and having a lot of money was part of the dream I wanted to attract. So, one day, I said, *"I got myself into a lot of debt, and I love myself anyway."*

Then, I cried. Unexpectedly, I cried because I felt a sense of relief, a sense of forgiveness, a feeling of worthiness. And it felt so good to love myself, in spite of the conditions in my life, even the bad ones I had created for myself.

I applied it to my body image, too. In my early twenties, I was a competitive bodybuilder. In bodybuilding, winning requires having a nearly perfect body. That's what the whole sport is about. Perfection. That did strange things to my self-esteem back when I was young. And since then, I've done a lot of things to stay in shape, always striving for perfection, never comfortable in my clothes if they're the least bit tight.

But one day, I was sitting on the couch, and I grabbed my thigh, a thigh I wanted less fat on, and more muscle, and I said, "I love myself, anyway." More tears. Because, in that moment, I realized how hard I'd been on myself, how I'd criticized myself too many times. But loving myself the way I was, in that moment, released so much tension... I swear, I might have lost five pounds of stress right then and there. *Poof.*

Funny thing, maintaining my preferred body composition got easier after that. By worrying about it less. The brain does weird things.

One more example. I had a headache one day. But instead of getting frustrated, I told my head that I loved it anyway. In spite of the headache, I love it. I even sent vibes of love to the headache itself. "Hi headache, I love you." Goofy, right? Well, a little relief and less tension followed those words and feelings, and after an hour, my headache lightened up. This is a powerful tip for healing. If you have hip pain, or back pain, or you stub your toe, instead of getting upset or frustrated with your body, tell that part of you that you love it anyway.

Why Does This Work?

Because love is an elevated emotion. Because loving yourself, as you are now, feels good. It's a kind of relief. It's a soothing balm on an otherwise racked nervous system. You'll elevate your emotions to help attract your magical life faster. And we heal faster when we reduce our stress, because stress causes inflammation, which wreaks havoc on the body.

You don't want to just love your future self. You want to love your *present self*—that's the one that matters!

Loving yourself, even when you don't feel lovable, drastically changes your vibe and the energy you put out. It cranks up your manifesting juju. It makes you happier, more focused, and productive, all of which make your dreams come true *much faster*.

Your Turn to Play!

Take a moment to think about things you've been wanting to change about yourself, or your life, or things you want to improve. Say each one out loud, and then immediately add,

I love myself anyway.

It might seem weird at first, but that's the cool part... it kinda catches you off-guard. Keep thinking and saying, "*I love myself anyway*," when thinking of things you want to change. Do this many times today, tomorrow, and the next day.

Make it your new habit, so that every time you're working on change, you're still loving yourself through it all.

You are loveable, always.

~

Today's affirmation:

I experience pleasure today, oodles and oodles of silky pleasure.

DAY 12: SWIMMING UPSTREAM

"Everybody in the world is seeking happiness—and there is one sure way to find it. That is by controlling your thoughts. Happiness doesn't depend on outward conditions. It depends on inner conditions."

— DALE CARNEGIE

Do you ever feel like you're swimming upstream? Even when you're working toward your goals and aspirations? Checking items off a never-ending to-do list? Well, *don't forget to be happy! Watch your thoughts! Be grateful! Find the silver lining!*

Sometimes it can feel like you're playing defense instead of offense.

But the truth is... living a magical life doesn't require constant defense. It doesn't require a mentality of *try, try, try.*

Yet, it still happens to all of us, the *swimming upstream* feeling. The feeling when you fear you'll be swept downstream and lose progress if you take a day off, or maybe even just rest for ten minutes.

Well, that's nonsense. Numerous studies have shown that people are more effective after taking a break. Or recharged after a vacation. And they often return with a new perspective. Or new ideas.

All from stepping away from things for a bit.

It's easy to get wrapped up working toward your goals and going after the life of your dreams. And in the process of chasing the magic, you can get so stressed that your life becomes completely devoid of... *magic!*

If this describes you, it's time to stop that.

Think about it... the recipe for living a magical life does not include ingredients of angst, over-effort, or tightness. You don't need to try so hard. That's swimming upstream. You know the feeling: *It's not relaxing, it's taxing.*

So here's a question for you: Is what you're doing to manifest your dreams taxing? Are you ever relaxing? Do you feel you're constantly pounding square pegs into round holes? Or slamming into a wall? You don't need to struggle so much. You don't need to force things so much, or interfere, like a well-meaning, nosy neighbor.

The problem with struggling too hard is that it wears you out. It makes you sloppy. It doesn't have to be like that. In fact, it shouldn't be like that, because struggle will always downshift your elevated emotions. If there's a moment when you feel like you're swimming upstream, that's the moment to let go, relax, and drift with the current. This will allow you to take a breath and recharge your batteries. Open up your mind and heart, and start generating all those wonderful, positive feelings.

Your progress won't cease; it will leap forward.

You see, you can move in the direction of your desires by thinking about and envisioning your exciting goals, and feeling elevated emotions, and then... *you can simply let go.* You can enjoy the flow of life. You can step aside, slow down, and let the process unfold. If you try too hard, think too hard, analyze too hard, such that it's a constant grind... then you risk blocking your own state of flow and abundance.

The great news is, you can be totally relaxed *and* go after your goals and dreams. Sometimes it helps to think of yourself as an *attractor.* Open your arms, your heart, and your mind and just... receive. No need to swim upstream. Let it all come to you.

It's about flowing, not forcing.

It's like kicking back in an inner tube and drifting gently down the river, not struggling against the current, attempting to make slow, agonizing progress headed upstream.

I used to swim hard against the current in my goal attempts, chasing something elusive. I don't even know exactly what. It was exhausting. Over the years, I've trained myself to relax and enter a kind of flow mode.

I mean, I still focus, and I still work... but without the struggle. I'm doing what I enjoy, pursuing the projects that speak to me at a personal level.

I turn away from things that don't feed my soul.

I take breaks.

As a result, I absolutely love what I'm doing—*every day*—and it doesn't *feel* like work. It feels like I'm playing. It's fun and uplifting. It's work only in the sense that downhill skiing or surfing is "work." It's a blast, and exhilarating, and at the end of the day, I sleep like a log.

It's a wonderful feeling. Every minute of it.

Your Turn to Play!

Write down the following three affirmations on sticky notes and place them where you'll see them (one affirmation per sticky note):

- *I am relaxed. I attract the life of my dreams.*
- *I no longer struggle to achieve the things I want. I open my arms, and they come to me.*
- *My life is easy and fun. I flow through it like a beautiful bird on a breeze.*

When you see these notes, remind yourself to relax and go with the flow, letting your dream and vision of the life you're designing come to you with your elevated thoughts and feelings.

You are fantastic!

~

Today's affirmation:

I elevate myself and my magnificence. I am worthy.

DAY 13: SPREADING COMPLIMENTS

"Always find opportunities to make someone smile, and to offer random acts of kindness in everyday life."

— Roy T. Bennett

I love giving compliments. To loved ones and strangers alike. You never know how much a simple compliment might turn someone's day around for the better, especially a compliment from a stranger. It's a free and easy way to inject some good into the world.

And it doesn't have to be awkward or weird. When you look at someone, you can find tons of ways to compliment them. You want to be genuine, of course, but it's easy to find something you like about someone. It could be her purse, or his necktie, or the way someone smiles, or styles their hair, or their eye color. Or something they do or say. There are so many opportunities to compliment people.

I remember one time I was in the gym, and there was a lady walking on the treadmill, looking like she'd rather be anywhere but there. She had short, blond hair, and she wore a bright aqua shirt. Despite looking a bit sad, her shirt really brightened her face. I went up to her and smiled and said, "That's a great color on you." And she beamed.

And her beaming made *me* feel great. That was a huge lesson. When you give compliments, the recipient isn't the only one who benefits. *You* feel good, too.

I was so moved by the whole encounter that, for the rest of the day, I looked for other people to compliment. I gave out a dozen compliments to total strangers. *It was amazing.* I knew I was making other people feel good, but it continued to blow me away by how good it made me feel. It's a total win-win!

Your Turn to Play!

Compliment four people today. Start with yourself right now... look in the mirror and find something to compliment yourself on.

For the other three, choose:

- someone in your family or household
- someone you know just a little (such as a coworker), and
- a stranger.

If you don't go out, then compliment these people online. You won't receive quite the same warm glow that you'd experience face-to-face, but that's ok.

If you're keeping a journal or notebook, write down the compliments you gave, and the resulting responses. Consider making this a regular behavior, or perhaps set a goal to give a certain number of compliments per day. And remember, be sure to make the compliments genuine. There's always something to compliment if you look carefully enough.

You are generous!

~

Today's affirmation:

Each day brings amazing new surprises.

DAY 14: RISE, SHINE, AND POWER UP

"Happiness depends upon ourselves."

— ARISTOTLE

It's Power Pose Time!

A *power pose* is basically you, standing like a superhero.

Why do this? For starters, it's fun. Even better, a Power Pose triggers self-confidence and a can-do attitude with a super effective shift in your mindset. Your posture influences your emotions, even little adjustments, like sitting up straight. So imagine what happens to your brain chemistry when you go *full Wonder Woman!*

Go ahead, try it!

When you strike a rad Power Pose, your body is telling your brain that you feel damn good about yourself. This is especially effective in times of self-doubt. The body takes charge of the situation, helping to convince your mind. Saying your Coffee Self-Talk in a Power Pose makes it even more effective.

Take advantage of this tiny neuro-hack today and increase your happiness and confidence. Change your body, change your state!

I love doing Power Poses. My kitchen in Italy has a door that opens and looks out over a courtyard. If I tip my chin up, I can see over the roof of the five-hundred-year-old building across the courtyard and the rolling hills beyond. I enjoy doing my Power Pose here. Sometimes I have my daughter take a picture of me from behind while I'm doing it. My Power Pose gives me a boost of energy and keeps me from sitting all the time. It boosts my confidence, too.

It's kind of like acting. Acting awesome.

And it makes you feel awesome.

Feeling good is the name of the game for living an incredible life. We want to *think amazing thoughts* and *feel elevated feelings* as often as possible. It's this combination that makes for powerful living.

> *Thoughts & Feelings.*
> *Thoughts & Feelings.*
> *Thoughts & Feelings.*

You want to be happy, live a glorious, magical life, and manifest everything you want. To make this happen, you want to feel good, as much as you can, all waking hours, whenever possible. And so, today, you're striking some Power Poses throughout the day to jazz up your feel-good chemicals in your body. This creates an amazing energy inside you, and around you, making you happy, and attracting great things.

Your Turn to Play!

Grab a timer and set it for two minutes. Then assume the position. My favorite is like a superhero: Hands on hips, eyes straight ahead, chin tilted up a bit, and a slight, knowing smile. You know the one, that knowing smile that shows you have the secrets, the power, and the answers. Yes! *Power up, people!*

And yes... two minutes! Don't stop until the timer goes off. If you feel goofy, that's fine. It will still work. *Have fun with it.*

While doing this, you can let your mind relax, and you can breathe in and out, feeling the energy of your badass self swirling around you.

Or, you can pick one of the following lines, and repeat it over and over, while striking your pose.

I am worthy.

I am love.

I am confident.

I am safe.

I am awesome.

Now, get your phone (or to-do list/calendar/notebook/etc.), and write the words *Power Pose* two times, for later in the day. If you can, set an alarm for these times.

Later on, when the alarm goes off, or you look at your to-do list and it's time, strike your Power Pose. If you're at work and don't want to do it in front of everyone, go use a bathroom stall, elevator, stairwell, or hallway. Pick one line from above and repeat it like a mantra for two minutes.

If you can't say your mantra out loud, then mouthing it silently is the next best thing. (Personally, I think it's awesome if you do it out loud in front of everyone, but you decide.)

Note: Power Poses are super effective for immediately inducing your most empowered state, such as before giving a presentation, taking a test, or any situation where you would benefit from boosted confidence. Teach this trick to your kids. Give them a cape. Heck, you wear a cape! Clip a long beach towel onto your shoulders.

Fake it to make it. Dress for success. Just do it! Have fun!

You are incredible!

∼

Today's affirmation:

I'm the master conductor of my own luminous life.

DAY 15: BRAIN BLUEPRINT

"You have to participate relentlessly in the manifestation of your own blessings."

— ELIZABETH GILBERT, *EAT, PRAY, LOVE*

"Brain Blueprints" are a powerful form of self-talk that you can do in little, one-minute increments at different times during the day. They're to the point, and they pack a punch. They're fun, too. (I mention these in the *Coffee Self-Talk Guided Journal*, but we'll go into a little more depth here because they're so effective.)

A Brain Blueprint is a descriptive, three-word, positive affirmation that catches your mind's attention and directs it to helping you make it become true. You give your brain a "blueprint" from which to work. A snappy, cool one.

Brain Blueprints use the following structure:

I am a [adjective], [adjective] [noun].

For example:

- I am a *Confident, Funny Genius.*
- I am an *Energetic, Fit Soul.*
- I am a *Funny, Lovable Mom.*

Because your brain is always listening, waiting for instructions on how to help you, Brain Blueprints are a way to keep those instructions front and center during the day, when you're not doing your regular Coffee Self-Talk.

The brilliant thing is that your brain *totally* wants to please you! It loves you so much that whatever you say or think, your brain takes as a command. I imagine my brain standing at attention, saluting me after everything I say, good or bad. *"Yes, ma'am! Will do, ma'am!"* (I'd better tell it to do good things!)

Remember, your brain doesn't care if what you tell it is the truth or a lie... it doesn't know the difference, and it will listen to whatever you say, whether it's good or bad, true or false, fiction or non-fiction. It will take the orders and start altering your body, moods, and actions for that result.

That's why your self-talk is vitally important.

So, Brain Blueprints are a specific way you can use your self-talk. You say these special, short affirmations in a trance-like, repetitive fashion, similar to a mantra. But they're punchy and fun, and powerful, like firecrackers.

Why Are Brain Blueprints Effective?

Here are two big reasons why Brain Blueprints work so well:

First, research has shown that our brains seek patterns, and we love things that come in three's. Groups of three feel "whole" to the brain, complete. And these Brain Blueprints fit the bill. They're catchy, like a slogan, so they're easy to remember.

Second, if you choose the right words, Brain Blueprints can also create an image. Your brain adores images, and it devotes extra space to remember them. And images are more powerful emotional triggers than words alone. We want those happy, elevated emotions because they raise our energy vibration, they can heal us, and they help us manifest our dreams faster. Lickety-split. Besides, don't we all just enjoy mind pictures? They're fun to imagine!

The idea for Brain Blueprints came to me one day when I was repeating the full-length affirmations,

I'm happy. I'm a happy person, and *I'm a millionaire. I'm wealthy. I'm rich.*

After repeating these several times, just for the heck of it, I blurted out, *"I'm a happy, sexy millionaire!"* And my brain went *ka-pow!... Happy Sexy Millionaire.* Now, that's punchy and memorable. It sounds like it's a thing, right?

There was so much packed into just three words... love, satisfaction, abundance, health, beauty, freedom... I could go on and on, but you get the idea, lots of material packed densely into three words.

Labels matter. When we label something, the brain takes notice, and gives that bucket of associations its own place in our view of the world. These three-word Brain Blueprints are custom labels you can create to give some group of things special meaning.

The image I created in my mind from this *Happy Sexy Millionaire* Brain Blueprint was a bright, colorful picture of me, smiling, wearing a big, sexy, movie star hat and sunglasses, with my makeup on point, stepping out of a limo at the ocean in the south of Italy. Now, *that's* a memorable image. It evokes emotion! It was vibrant and fun. It was *electrifying*.

Aim for a similar *electric sizzle* as you try on a few different Brain Blueprints for size. You can use whatever words you want, but taken together, the phrase should *speak to you*.

Now, before I give some more examples, I want to be clear: Brain Blueprints do *not* replace your regular Coffee Self-Talk. That said, you can include some Brain Blueprints within your Coffee Self-Talk. Your daily Coffee Self-Talk is a more fluid, more flowing experience. It provides a space for both big ideas and small ideas. Not just punchy positive affirmations, but also long, flowery, and glittery thoughts and feelings of love and awe.

Brain Blueprints add little firecracker affirmations easily to your day. Because they're written in such a way as to make them more effective and easy to remember, they can be used while you're doing other things, so your mind doesn't wander. It's an easy way to inject more powerful affirmations into your life.

Here are a few more examples...

I am a *Funny, Lovable Manager.*

I am a *Sexy, Strong Creator.*

I am a *Patient, Funny Mom.*

I am a *Generous, Intuitive Teacher.*

I am a *Happy, Generous Millionaire.*

I am a *Bright, Healthy Painter.*

I am a *Confident, Luminescent Artist.*

I am a *Strong, Intuitive Manifester.*

I am a *Beautiful, Intuitive Entrepreneur.*

I am a *Sexy, Intuitive Writer.*

I am a *Healthy, Creative Woman.*

I am a *Fit, Prolific Genius.*

Notice how some of these combinations aren't very intuitive? How they hit your brain a little sideways? I mean, *sexy* and *writer* aren't usually uttered together. But they work, and it makes your brain do a little double take. *I love it!*

Your Turn to Play!

Write some Brain Blueprints for yourself. Think of a variety of words to describe the new you that you're becoming, or that you want to become. Mix them up and write down a few combinations.

Once you've written down a few, pick your favorite one, write it on six sticky notes, and place them where you'll see them. Then add it to your phone (or to-do list/calendar/notebook/etc.) and set a reminder to show it to you several times a day.

Every time you see the stickies and reminders, use them as a trigger to say the phrase a few times. Also repeat your chosen Brain Blueprint while you're doing mindless physical activities, like cleaning dishes, cooking, making coffee, doing reps at the gym, walking, brushing your hair, painting your nails, or whatever. Do this softly for one to two minutes each time you see one of your reminders, and you'll find that they create a satisfying emotional response as they start to settle in, as though they're finding their new home inside you.

For greater effect, keep those elevated emotions soaring. Actually try to *feel* what it would feel like for your Brain Blueprint to become true!

You can say them powerfully, out loud, with gusto and verve! Your mind really listens up when you put more energy into something, and saying it out loud gets the brain's attention. If you're standing in line at the bank, or around people at work, you can just whisper it. Even mouthing the words helps them work their way into the grooves of your mind.

And lastly, a fantastic time to saturate your subconscious with powerful words like this is just before you go to sleep. Repeat your Brain Blueprint when your head hits the pillow, and fall to sleep as you repeat it softly.

You are a shining miracle of grace and potential.

Today's affirmation:

I feel it now, a new sun rising inside me and radiating out, beyond, farther than I've ever been. Yeaaahh!

DAY 16: BIG LOVE TRIGGERS

"I'm happy. Which often looks like crazy."

— DAVID HENRY HWANG

What really makes you gush love? What stirs you so profoundly that the emotion practically brings you to your knees? What moves your soul, whipping it into a vortex of love and energy so strong that the emotion cracks your heart right open? What makes you feel a warmth and energy so profound, you feel you could light up a city with it?

When you feel big love for anything, it makes you happier, reduces stress, and comforts you. You might feel it from being in nature, witnessing the birth of a baby, petting a puppy, hearing certain music, witnessing generosity, or helping others. It makes your soul take flight and fills you with awe. That feeling is the elevated emotion of love. And every time you feel it, it attracts more love to you. It's magnificent. It's wondrous.

Feeling this level of emotion on a regular basis will make your life more special. *More magical.* It will empower you, make you giggle, and take your life to new heights.

Big Love Experiences

Today's fun exercise helps you learn how to tap into that elevated emotion more quickly, by thinking about things that reliably create this effect in you.

For me, I get this feeling in a few different ways. I feel it in nature. I feel it when I see those viral videos of people rescuing wild animals caught in traps or mud. I also feel it when I watch YouTube videos of Dr. Joe Dispenza's healing retreats. When the emotion stirs in my chest, I notice it, and I try to anchor the feeling, trying to *really* remember it, so I can call it up on a moment's notice at any time in the future. Sometimes it's easier to summon this feeling during the first few days after having a *Big Love* experience. But the more times you recall the feeling, the longer it stays with you, and the easier it is to repeat.

Once you have some examples in your mind—or even just one example—of things that give you a feeling of Big Love —this elevated emotional state—bring up that picture in your mind (or listen to that special music, or rewatch that tingle-inducing YouTube video), and try to actually *feel* the love. Deep down, with no holding back. You want to burn that feeling into your memory, and tap into it as often as you can.

It may take you a while to find your Big Love trigger. If you're having trouble thinking of something that made you feel this way, go back as far in time as you need to. It doesn't need to be something recent. That said, if you can think of something recent, that's good, because the memory will be clearer and emotionally stronger.

If you still can't think of anything, then think of a time when you just felt great, or you had a strong feeling of love, and focus on that. The key is to identify the thing that made you feel good. If nothing at all comes to mind, then tuck this exercise away for a bit, and be on the lookout for experiences that give you that great sense of emotion, wonder, and awe.

When you feel it, you'll know it! Memorize that feeling. Think about it, experience it fully in your mind.

Once you come up with one thing that consistently opens your heart and makes the love pour out, write it down someplace where you'll see it (a sticky note, your notebook, phone, etc.).

Attempt to recall this feeling 2-3 times a day for the next few days. Every time you see your sticky note (or other reminder), take a moment, and draw that feeling into your body to relive the experience and the elevated emotional state. If appropriate, close your eyes, and let the feeling of love fill you. Relish in your wonderful feelings, and carry them throughout your day.

Once you've gotten good at recalling your Big Love feeling, you'll have this tool for the rest of your life, to use whenever you like.

You are love!

～

Today's affirmation:

It is safe to follow my truth, my love, my creativity, my inspirations. My heart is always safe.

DAY 17: I PREFER VS. I HOPE

"Laughter is a sunbeam of the soul."

— THOMAS MANN

Once upon a time, I was a vegan. I died. The End.

Just kidding.

Yes, I was a vegan for ten years, until it almost killed my family.

Ok, I'm being dramatic again. (Maybe.)

I'm bringing up my days as a vegan because, back in those wheatgrass-soaked days, I read a book that had a gem of an idea that I've carried with me, over a decade later. This strange and peculiar book, *Survival in the 21st Century*, was written by an odd and truly enjoyable fella with amazing, huge ears, Viktoras Kulvinskas.

When I finished the book, I cut out a little chart from it and taped it into my journal. And over the years, as I moved from journal to journal, I would re-tape the chart into all of my journals. Until I internalized it, I guess, because I don't have it anymore.

I won't attempt to reconstruct the whole table here, but I'll share the general idea. It's a simple idea. But a powerful one.

Take the words, *"I hope,"* and never use them again. Strike this word combination from your vocabulary.

And then replace them with the words, *"I prefer."*

Every time.

I prefer. I prefer. I prefer. I prefer.

I started doing this, and I was baffled at the difference in my reaction. The difference in the feeling of hoping for something, versus preferring it, was startling. *Why was this?* Well, when you say *I prefer*, there is less attachment to it, yet more agency and personal power. In a weird way, it's more uplifting, like you're in charge. There's a feeling of *untouchableness* that accompanies the words, *"I prefer."* And it works.

Hope is the opposite. When you hope, you're at the mercy of everything *but* you.

I was teaching this idea to my 10-year-old daughter, and I asked her what she thought about it. She said, *"Yeah, it sounds more educated."*

So there.

But, seriously. Try the magic for yourself. Try it for everything you *prefer* to happen in your life. You know, the positive stuff, the things you *hope* for.

For example, when driving your car, instead of saying, "I *hope* I make this green light," say, "I *prefer* to make this green light."

Ahhh, doesn't that just feel better? Feeling soft and pink, like cotton candy?

This is not trivial. Words matter. Precision with our words leads to precision in our thinking.

Another example: "I *hope* to lose weight." No. Try this instead... "I *prefer* to lose weight." So much nicer, like slipping into a nice, warm, rose-scented bubble bath.

And then also use this clever linguistic hack for everything that you *don't* want—that you *prefer* doesn't happen.

For example: "I *hope* I don't get sick." Nope. Try... "I *prefer* not to get sick." More empowering, right? Like, kinda badass.

There's less stress behind *I prefer* than *I hope*. A more elevated feeling, more relaxation, less attachment to outcomes. And that is magnificently powerful.

Your Turn to Play!

Take a moment and close your eyes. Think of something that you would like to have happen.

Now say it out loud, in the following form (fill in the blank with the thing you want to happen),

I hope that _____.

Now change "hope" to "prefer," and say it aloud again, in this new form,

I prefer that _____.

Do you notice how this makes you feel differently about it? A little less desperate sounding? It's as though your happiness is no longer dependent on getting the desired outcome. That's powerful.

Going forward, make it a point to use *prefer* instead of *hope*.

Grab a few sticky notes, and write "I prefer" on them, as a reminder. Stick them around your house for the next week. This weird little hack really works!

You are miraculous!

∼

Today's affirmation:

I love and approve of myself, one million percent.

DAY 18: 5-MINUTE BLISSFUL MOVEMENT TIME

"You must be the best judge of your own happiness."

— JANE AUSTEN

Today is a day for movement. Just five minutes of it. Movement makes us feel good. Movement is inspiring. You're going to whip up some bliss, right now, by moving energy, breathing, and adding a glimmery zest to your day. Remember, uplifted thoughts, when cooked with elevated emotions, are key ingredients to your magnificent manifesting recipe.

Ideas for Your 5-Minutes of Blissful Movement

Walking

The repetitive motion that occurs while walking triggers a beautiful relaxation response in your body. When this happens, stress dissipates like the fog under a hot sun, and you simultaneously get a boost in energy to accompany your uplifted mood. The bilateral motion of walking benefits our brains in remarkable ways. Plus? You get in extra steps for the day!

Stretching

I love stretching; it's simply glorious! With each body part, a stretch feels like a delicious hug for that part. Equally cool is that stretching can release happy chemicals (endorphins), so you're automatically going to like it.

When you do a mild stretch, it increases circulation throughout your body. Be mindful not to stretch too far and harm yourself! Don't stretch if it's painful. The goal is not to stretch hard, but rather, to seek a mild pulling that *feels good* as it releases tightness. And remember that toes, hands, arms and feet can stretch, too. Breathe deeply through each part your stretch.

Yoga: Sun Salutation

If you're into yoga, you can also flow through a sun salutation, or any moves of your choice. It's a great way to combine stretching and movement. If you're not familiar with this, just search for "yoga sun salutation" on YouTube for a quick lesson.

Dancing

This is one of my favorite ways to move. I frequently don my headphones—usually once or twice a day—and dance my heart out around the kitchen, no matter who is with me. Dancing makes me feel powerful.

Mantras + Movement

And while you're walking or stretching, repeat one or two of your favorite lines of your Coffee Self-Talk. I love the constant repetition of,

> *I am worthy. I am loved.*

Or,

> *I am living my most magical life.*
> *I am worthy of all my heart's desires.*

Over and over, thinking these thoughts, feeling beautiful, juicy feelings, and smiling. Because you are amazing!

Your Turn to Play!

Set a timer for five minutes, get up, and do some movement right now. You can walk if you like... around your kitchen table, up and down your stairs, or go outside. Or stretch, or do yoga. Or do ten squats, a thirty-second plank, some crunches, and some jumping jacks. You only need five minutes. It's a tiny amount of time to move and self-talk-mantra your way into a lovely day.

Extra credit: Write *"5-Minute Blissful Movements"* on a few sticky notes, and post them around your house as a reminder. You can do this exercise more times throughout the day for a brilliant reset, a moment for you, and a surge in endorphins and happiness, all of which help you manifest your fantastic plans faster...

while feeling great. Think *and* feel amazing, and your life will be amazing.

Change your energy, and you'll change your life.

You are magnificent.

~

Today's affirmation:

I attract the most amazing life of friends, experiences, awe, love, and riches, because I'm so worth it.

DAY 19: MEET YOUR ROOMMATE

"The greater part of our happiness or misery depends upon our dispositions, and not upon our circumstances."

— MARTHA WASHINGTON

Do you ever notice how you go through your day narrating it as it occurs? You could be getting into your car, and it's like words and thoughts go through your head directing you to *put the keys in the ignition,* and then, *oh the seat is uncomfortable,* then *who drove this last time and didn't put the seat back?*

You pull out of the garage and start further narrating in your head, *Oh the weather is rainy, I didn't bring an umbrella. What am I having for lunch today? My waistband feels tight, I shouldn't have eaten that pasta last night. Maybe if I skip lunch, I'll lose a pound. What am I making for dinner tonight?*

And on and on.

Fairly neutral stuff, but still chatty.

And then, sometimes, that voice in your head isn't very nice to you. And you let it be like that. Of course, with self-talk, you know that the words you think and feel are paramount to living your best life, and your morning Coffee Self-Talk is changing that. Good job! But still... you can get caught up in life, narrating every step, passing judgment about each step as you go, and just overall not living a peaceful, flowy life, due to the constant *blah blah blah*.

Now, imagine this voice is your roommate (props to author Michael Singer for the idea).

A roommate in *your* house.

Gah! It would be so damn annoying to be forced to listen to this roommate narrating, non-stop, every little thing you do, judging, criticizing, analyzing, or just making mindless chatter. We all do it. But when you think of this voice as a roommate, you might suddenly feel like giving it the stink eye, or even a middle finger once in a while!

You might also find it rather fascinating, when you really think about it... that a roommate is living inside your head. And when you spend a day listening to it, you'll find yourself blown away by all the incessant chatter competing for your time and energy. All too often, the roommate is there... fueling fire, ratcheting up irritation, or just plain distracting you while you're trying to chill out, or even fall asleep.

Or is the roommate just playing devil's advocate, challenging you to consider all the angles and avoid mistakes?

To be fair, the roommate is probably just trying to be helpful. Trouble is, the roommate doesn't always know what's best for us. And the chatter can overwhelm and drown out the quieter, more subtle voice of your intuition.

The roommate might be trying to help, but life is not as fragile as the roommate sharing space in your mind would have you believe. You might not ever silence the roommate (and I'm not sure you'd want to evict it permanently), but turning the volume down on your roommate's chatter 50% might do wonders for your sense of peace.

Good news! Now that you're aware of the presence of your roommate, it'll now be easier to recognize when it's not helping you. This will give you some peace and help you catch some of the times you might otherwise have entered negative self-talk territory. The more you catch these times, the easier it is to correct course. You'll become skilled at noticing the thoughts and letting them go, rather than blindly following them down the path of negativity.

You can do like Luca, in the Disney movie *Luca*, when he yells to his fearmongering mental roommate, *"Silencio, Bruno!"* (Luca named his mental roommate.)

When I started actively listening to the roommate in my head, I quickly noticed when she was most opinionated. She was always blathering on about what I ate or whether I should be on a diet. *Jeez! What a wench.* But I've caught her enough times now and stopped her in her tracks. She's no longer riding shotgun in my head. I relegated her to the back seat where she belongs.

And today? Because I'm all about having as much love and juicy, high vibe energy in my life... instead of giving my roommate the middle finger when she tries to push her way into my life, now I blow her a kiss and say, *bye-bye, honey!*

Your Turn to Play!

Your mission on this beautiful day is to pay attention to your inner dialog. Is your roommate saying nice things? Neutral? Negative?

Also notice what songs you listen to, the things you say to yourself, the shows you watch, the way you feel on social media. Are these making you feel marvelous about yourself and your life? If so, great! Keep it up.

If not, take note. You may wish to start correcting these inputs to your thinking immediately, but if all you do is notice the effect they're having for the next few days, that's a great first step toward living your magical life.

You rock.

❧

Today's affirmation:

Love. It's my solution. Always. Love.

DAY 20: LINK MASSIVE PLEASURE TO EVERYTHING

"The more you praise and celebrate your life, the more there is in life to celebrate."

— OPRAH WINFREY

Today is a fun day. You're going to link massive pleasure to everything big and small that you like or feel good about.

Your massive pleasure is going to be *explosive.* Every time you see, hear, or think about something you like, you'll react as if the team you're rooting for just made the winning goal of the championship game! You would jump out of your seat, punch your fist in the air, and whoop and holler and yell. We're going after that kind of pleasure.

Why? Because it's silly, fun, and effective.

I'll go first.

Let's take coffee. I will presume that most of you like your coffee as much as I do. Or maybe it's your tea, or your kombucha, or your sparkling water. You like it a lot, but do you ever actually give it the enthusiasm it deserves? Today, you will. As you make your coffee, say to your delicious coffee, "*Oh my gawd! Coffee! I love you sooooooo much! You are amazing!*"

You get a green light while driving... "*YEAH BABY! I Go and I flow! I love you, green light!!!*"

You're transferring a bag of flour into a container... "*OMGoodness! I love this! Flour is awesome! I love you, flour!*"

A song comes on you love... "*Song! You! I love you so much! You are such an incredible song!*"

You glob toothpaste onto your toothbrush. Be in awe of it. Look at it as it squirts out of the tube. Study it like you're from an alien planet. You've never seen *anything* so interesting. "*Wow! I LOVE THIS! Toothpaste, you are amaze-balls. I love you so much!*"

You see your reflection in the mirror. "*You! You! You! I love you so very, very much! I love you! You're fantastic! Damn, I just love the hell out of you!*"

I'm serious... do it for practically everything. Cool stuff. Mundane stuff. All stuff.

Go over the top, like chocolate-covered-sprinkles-sweetness over the top!

OMG, I LOVE THIS!

All. Day. Long.

When you turn your focus to things that you normally take for granted, you start to experience the world with childlike wonder. Everything was amazing to you the first time you saw it. Water, the sunset, a dog, a horse, a smart phone. Think about it... the only reason these aren't amazing every day is because you've grown accustomed to them. You have become blind to their awesomeness.

This exercise gives you sight again. Your *original vision*. It's a special type of mindfulness, and a special type of gratitude. Mindful because you're focusing on things you've not focused on in a long time. Grateful because you're appreciating just how amazing they are.

In fact, all gratitude is a special kind of mindfulness.

By repeating the exercise multiple times, with multiple things, you can start to build the *habit of awareness*, noticing more, witnessing beauty, and experiencing awe. And the more often, and the more ways you can experience awe, the more magical your life will become, both right now, and in the future, as you draw your dream life to you ever faster.

You see the world through new eyes every day!

Today's affirmation:

Oh-My-Gawd! I'm awesome!!

DAY 21: IT'S COMING TO ME!

"Your success and happiness lie in you."

— HELEN KELLER

There's something interesting about repeating a mantra about something that you want. It's kind of hypnotic and relaxing, and it's one of my favorite things to do for manifesting. It keeps my mind from wandering or getting distracted with unhelpful thoughts. It's relaxing, too.

But perhaps the most interesting thing about repeating a *manifestation mantra* is that... *you start to believe it.* You get this groovy sort of feeling of *knowing,* of *expectancy,* of *rightness,* that comes over you. This feeling that it's actually going to happen, and that everything will just magically work out somehow.

And speaking of relaxation... mantras are relaxing in general, but there's something extra relaxing about repeating your manifestation mantra. The relaxation comes from the expectation that's created inside you, that what you want is coming. It's a peaceful, comforting feeling, like all of your fears and anxiety about the future just wash away.

It's a strange and powerful exercise.

When I first started playing around with this exercise, I started with the line,

Millions of dollars are coming to me.

(I'm not suggesting that I only cared about money. Nothing could be further from the truth. It's just that I was already happy, healthy, and had a lot of love, adventure, and creative outlets in my life, and so making serious bucks was just kinda the next thing on my to-do list.)

Anyway, I just kept softly repeating it over and over one day, while I was sitting on the couch staring at the wall.

Millions of dollars are coming to me.
Millions of dollars are coming to me.
Millions of dollars are coming to me.

I said it on my inhale and again on my exhale. Over and over. Sometimes with my eyes closed, sometimes with them open. I don't even know how long I sat there doing it.

And this interesting feeling of lovely comfort washed over me. So I played with it more and did it many times throughout that day. I repeated the mantra when I was cooking or washing my hands (COVID-style, 20 seconds). Sometimes, I said it out loud, and my family heard me (they like when I do things like this, experimenting with my weird shit).

It was very powerful.

Why is this simple activity so effective? It's effective, and important, because the lovely, cozy feeling that I was experiencing was a form of elevated emotions. I wasn't feeling survival emotions (fear, anxiety, or scarcity), and I wasn't feeling any lack. *I was feeling total peace.* And having peace of mind is a required part of the formula for living a magical life.

As of this writing, I don't yet have millions of dollars in my bank account. But my income has increased dramatically, which I attribute to everything I do with my morning *Coffee Self-Talk* and the exercises in this book. And more importantly, I *feel like a million bucks*, every day.

Now, while you're doing your mantra... that's not the time to think about *how* or *why* you'll manifest the thing you seek. It's not the time for planning, or doubts, or questions. Rather, it's a time for *knowing*, and *expecting*, and really, just saying the words. Saying them opens your mind and heart for your desired future to appear in any fashion. It's part of the *Grand Mystery*. It's also part of what makes it sooooo deliciously relaxing... you're just chilling in a lovely little hypnotic state, with no pressure to try and figure anything out.

Your Turn to Play!

Think of something you want: love, connection, excitement, purpose, money, security, happiness, a bangin' body, a specific healing. I know, they all sound good, *right?* Pick just one for today's focus. You can choose another one another day.

On six sticky notes, write the following:

_____ *is coming to me!*

Insert the thing you want in the blank space. Then add it to your phone (or to-do list/calendar/notebook/etc.). The point is having this in multiple places to remind you.

Every time you see one of your notes or reminders, take 60 seconds, and say out loud:

_____ *is coming to me.*

Set a timer, if you like. For extra relaxation, you can say it while breathing in, and repeat it while breathing out, to make it like a breathing mantra. Or you could say it out loud while striking a Power Pose (see Day #14). Or you can say it with a smile, you can say it softly, or you can silently mouth the words while standing in line at the grocery store.

The sticky notes and calendar notes are dedicated reminders, but you can also say your mantra anytime you're doing things that don't require your total focus, like cooking or prepping food. With every peel of the potato, say it like a mantra.

You are terrific!

~

Today's affirmation:

I'm a master at manifesting. I show up to my life, every day.

DAY 22: NO NEWS DAY

"Children are happy because they don't have a file in their minds called 'All the Things That Could Go Wrong.'"

— MARIANNE WILLIAMSON

Today, the game is taking a break from the news. No news feeds, no TV.

Don't worry, the world will go on... but without your worrying. The news is rarely positive and uplifting, so taking a break from it can do loads for keeping your emotions elevated.

According to Time Magazine,

"More than half of Americans say the news causes them stress, and many report feeling anxiety, fatigue or sleep loss as a result. Yet one in 10 adults checks the news every hour, and fully 20% of Americans report 'constantly' monitoring

their social media feeds—which often exposes them to the latest news headlines, whether they like it or not."

So you might abstain from social media today, too.

According to the American Psychological Association,

> *"Adults also indicated that they feel conflicted between their desire to stay informed about the news and their view of the media as a source of stress. While most adults (95 percent) say they follow the news regularly, 56 percent say that doing so causes them stress, and 72 percent believe the media blows things out of proportion."*

Graham Davey, professor emeritus of psychology at Sussex University in the UK, has research showing that,

> *"Negative TV news is a significant mood-changer, and the moods it tends to produce are sadness and anxiety."*

And according to The Guardian, the media *exaggerates negative news.* Why? Because *"if it bleeds, it leads."* The vast majority of the news is negative because fear motivates most people, and they literally can't resist clicking and watching. It's all about advertising revenue. Money.

Welp, not me.

I don't make space for that crap in my life. I'm too mindful of my uplifted state. I'm too happy, and I'm not willing to let anything useless cut into that. I'm a fierce unicorn, manifesting my Happy Sexy Millionaire life with glitter and starbursts, and I'll be damned if I'm going to delay that happening even one day. I don't need to follow the latest celebrity gossip, or listen to some politician evade questions and spin B.S.

Call me when we clone a T-Rex, ok? Now *that*, I'd watch!

There's this thing called *negativity bias*, which means people tend to pay more attention to negative stuff than positive stuff.

That is, *unless you're doing Coffee Self-Talk.*

I could go on and on with research findings and examples. It's a fascinating topic, really. But I want to get to the next point, the important reason that taking a break from news is good for you.

The bottom line: You need to take control over your information diet. Ruthlessly. What you watch and read literally wires your brain. If negative things automatically draw a large audience, and if we're seeing that all this negativity in the news is having a bad impact on us, then I say it's time to take a break. A fast from negative news... which is almost *all* news. Do it cold turkey for a day (or week or month).

Then, fill your brain with happiness, and let your heart burst with elevated emotions, as you rewire your brain to *seek the positive!* That's how I live. I never seek negative, and I don't put more weight on negative things. No way, no how. My glass is always half full, I see silver linings, and I love being happy.

As I shared in *Coffee Self-Talk*, I hardly ever watch the news. Like, never. And I don't feel uninformed. Most news is not relevant to my life. But if anything important happens, I hear about it from those in my sphere who follow it closely, and whom I trust to be good information filters.

The important stuff always makes it through my filter. And items related to my interests come to me through social media (friends, Twitter, etc.). When I hear about something that's important to me, I investigate to learn more. So, it's not that I receive no information—I consume quite a lot, actually—it's just that I impose a very high bar on what's allowed to enter my brain.

If it's likely to harm me, I don't let it in.

When I turned off the news, the increase in my clarity, mindset, creativity, peace, and happiness skyrocketed. It freed me from so much daily distraction.

Your Turn to Play!

This one is easy. No news today.

Or go big, and avoid it for a whole week!

And, of course, if you're really serious about manifesting your dreams, maintaining elevated emotions, and living a magical life, then set a reminder on your calendar to fast from the news regularly. Maybe for one week each month, as a start! And, if people want to talk about the news during your news fast, then give them a big sloppy grin and say, "No thanks, I'm on a *no-news diet* this week!"

You are resilient.

❧

Today's affirmation:

I slice through the mundane to reveal the marvelous. I am empowered.

DAY 23: GRATITUDE IMMUNE SYSTEM BOOSTER

"My God, a moment of bliss. Why, isn't that enough for a whole lifetime?"

— FYODOR DOSTOEVSKY

Gratitude can significantly boost your happiness, and that's what we're doing today. Healthy bodies. Healthy minds. Healthy lives!

When you experience gratitude, signals from your brain calm your nervous system, making you feel more relaxed. That means spending less time in survival mode, or with negative emotions. As you might expect, being thankful makes you feel elevated emotions, and these elevated emotions and feelings have direct physical benefits, like healing.

Gratitude does the body good! When you're grateful, your cells get busy boosting your immune system. Robert A. Emmons, professor of psychology at UC Davis, reports that gratitude lowers blood pressure and improves immune function. It even facilitates better, more efficient sleep, which plays a huge role in preventing sickness.

If I get sick, or if I'm around sick people, my first line of defense is *gratitude, gratitude, gratitude.* I close my eyes and feel myself being flooded with appreciation. I feel appreciation for my legs and the ability to walk. I squeeze them while I think it. I feel appreciation for my vision and sight, and I open my eyes and take in all the details around me. I give thanks for the food and drink that passes my lips on those days. Frankly, it should be every day, but it doesn't always happen.

Then, I reach for my zinc lozenges, green or peppermint tea, and vitamin C. And as I take each one, I repeat heartfelt feelings of gratitude for having them. (This one is easy. When I traveled, these items were not always easy to find. Having them on hand always makes me feel a small sense of security.)

Now that you know that deliberately expressing gratitude can fend off disease, you have a trick up your sleeve, should you happen to find yourself around sick people, or if you get sick yourself.

Even better, be proactive about it, before you get sick or come into contact with people's cooties. Having a "Day of Gratitude," as I suggest below, is the perfect way to give your health and immune system a boost!

Your Turn to Play!

Write *I Am Grateful* on six sticky notes, and place them where you'll see them. Then add it to your phone (or to-do list/calendar/notebook/etc.).

Every time you see one of these notes, look around and think about something that you are indeed grateful about. Give thanks for it in your heart. Feel appreciation for having it in your life, and smile while you're at it. :)

You may feel a small sense of calm when you do this. But what you might not feel directly, is that your immune system just got a little boost, too.

You are strong and healthy!

～

Today's affirmation:

I am grateful for my body, my home, my clothes, my mindset, my power, my love.

DAY 24: CHILLAXED MANIFESTING

"It's a helluva start, being able to recognize what makes you happy."

— LUCILLE BALL

There's a large element of surrender in manifesting your dreams. Instead of the thinking... *Go Go Go!*, it's more like... *Think. Feel. Chill. Relax.*

Relaxation is part of the manifesting recipe. It's surrendering your ideas and plans to something greater than yourself. It keeps you open. It keeps your energy positive. And manifesting is all about your energy.

When we *Go Go Go*, we tire ourselves out. We can become so focused that we don't have an open mind. This puts blinders on us. You can become so focused, you miss opportunities, solutions, and better routes to get you where you want to go. Or someplace you hadn't even imagined.

What Else Can It Do?

When you're in a Go Go Go mindset, and not relaxing, there exists a kind of tension, which is not a positive emotion. It may feel exciting or stressful, but tension comes from the part of your nervous system that's geared toward survival. And so when you take time to relax and let the universe and energy work in your favor, work *for* you, your struggle ceases, and a rooted peace soothes the nerves in your body.

I had to learn to relax my manifesting for business success. That doesn't mean I sat on the couch all day, eating delicious bonbons, just thinking and feeling magnificent feelings while the sales rolled in. But it also didn't mean I ran like a racehorse all day long, trying to hammer my manifestations into being. Instead, I did my Coffee Self-Talk each morning, taking my time, giving it the space that it deserves. I thought and felt beautiful things all day, and then I'd do some good, solid work—in my relaxed state—and then when I was done, I was done. I didn't keep checking my email, I relaxed. I surrendered. This allowed my mindset to remain open and positive and expecting great things, but I wasn't cracking whips to make it happen.

Did my chillaxed approach work? Yes.

Surprisingly well, actually. I was extremely productive, my business thrived, and—here's the slightly mystical part— even the things beyond my control seemed to somehow just "come together" easier. Like total strangers contacting me out of the blue, such as to book interviews or inquire about licensing foreign rights to my books.

Would these inquiries have come in if I'd been in my Go Go Go mindset? Maybe. But one thing's for sure, I would not have been in the same peaceful state of mind when I responded to them, and that makes a huge difference.

So chillax, and let the universe do its thing.

Your Turn to Play!

Write *Surrender* or *Chillax* on three sticky notes. Then get your phone (or to-do list/calendar/notebook/etc.) and add the word there, too. Place the stickies someplace where you'll see them.

Later today, every time you see your reminders, take a breath, keep your vibe high, and *relax*. Surrender the thoughts and work you're doing to manifest your dreams. Surrender, knowing that it's an ebb and flow of energy—a *dance with the universe*—and that it's all coming to you, because you're an amazing, beautiful, deserving person.

You are a creative genius.

Today's affirmation:

I keep one foot in the physical, and one foot in the metaphysical. The space between these two is where I create.

DAY 25: CONSTANT CREATING

"Creativity doesn't wait for that perfect moment. It fashions its own perfect moments out of ordinary ones."

— BRUCE GARRABRANDT

When I was growing up, my mom always said to me, *Throw enough shit on the wall, and something will stick.*

Today's list is about writing down ideas for how you can keep on moving, regarding your creativity, personal projects, and career. The idea is that, once you create or complete something, you jump straight to creating or doing the next thing, and then the next, and the next. Create, and then let it go. Create again, and let it go.

What does this mean?

It means you become a *Constant Creator*. You don't get stagnant. You don't stop. You always ask, "What next?"

So again... create, and then let it go. Don't get caught up in how it's received, or how successful it is. Just create, let it go, and move on.

As an author, this is part of my process. Write, publish, write, publish. I just keep creating. I don't get caught up wondering how well a book is doing. I don't get side-tracked reading reviews all day. Once I put something out there, it means I've let it go, and it's time to move on to the next project.

It's better to look forward and create something new than constantly glancing in the rearview mirror. In other words, you keep on moving.

You keep giving yourself more times at bat, more chances for success.

You keep throwing stuff on the wall.

Even if you don't intend to make money from your creations, using this *Constant Creator* philosophy leads to a continuous flow of creative output, keeping you engaged, growing, and always working toward a goal. And these are essential to long-term happiness, and even long life!

It doesn't matter what form your creativity takes—journaling, knitting, cooking, woodworking, painting, music, building websites, gardening, you name it—just keep on doing it.

So, for instance, suppose you wanted to take up drawing in your spare time... once you finish a sketch, you'd start the next one, and the next one, and then the next one. Just keep moving. Keep creating.

Your Turn to Shine!

Write a list of all the different things you could create, or that you'd like to experiment with, to see if you like it.

Try to list as many things as you can.

Ready, set... *GO!*

You are a blazing, prosperous being.

~

Today's affirmation:

I have time to do everything I want today. Time is abundant. My creativity is abundant.

DAY 26: A DAY OF GLORIOUS SIMPLICITY

"Our life is frittered away by detail. Simplify, simplify."

— HENRY DAVID THOREAU

How can you simplify, just for today?

We live in a world of mind-numbing choices and decisions to be made. Step inside any large grocery store, and you'll be blinded by all the colors and the staggering options, all vying for your attention. It can drain you. You might think choices are good, and that they represent a type of freedom. Sometimes they do. But sometimes the old saying rings true:

Too much of anything is not a good thing.

Too many choices can lead to *decision-making fatigue*, which increases stress, while simultaneously sucking the energy from you like a vampire.

Decision-making fatigue is the mental and emotional strain that taxes you when you have too many decisions to make and options to choose from. Too many decisions can lead to getting overstressed, and then people can become hasty, making worse decisions, or putting off making the decision entirely. There's a biological price for having so many decisions to make. It saps your energy. In fact, a lot of online shopping carts are abandoned when the shopper is presented with too many choices. You throw up your hands and your brain shuts down. You jump ship.

The problem is not just that you have five hundred boxes of cereal to choose from in the cereal aisle. It's the accumulation of all the decisions you have to make all day long. What time should I wake up? Should I hit snooze? What do I wear today? What color lipstick do I choose? Should I wear perfume? What do I eat for breakfast? Do I stop for gas on the way to work? Do I exercise today? What kind of exercise do I do? How long should I do it? What's for dinner? And on and on…

Decision-making fatigue doesn't only affect regular folks, it also causes professionals to make bad decisions. According to the New York Times Magazine article, *Do You Suffer from Decision Fatigue?*,

> *"This sort of decision fatigue can make quarterbacks prone to dubious choices late in the game and C.F.O.'s prone to disastrous dalliances late in the evening. It routinely warps the judgment of everyone, executive and non-executive, rich and poor."*

When I first learned about decision-making fatigue, and how Steve Jobs only wore black shirts so he'd have one less decision to make each day, it inspired me! (Jobs actually got the idea from Einstein.) I'm a "go big or go home" kind of gal, so when I heard this idea, I tore through my closet with gusto, like a glittering tornado, getting rid of tons of stuff. I rifled through my makeup drawer and paired down to only the minimum of color choices. Having fewer lipsticks, believe it or not, created a noticeable reduction in decision-making fatigue. Not life-changing, but combined with a few other small changes, these added up to a significant improvement in my daily life.

Simplify!

And then there was the time I went on a 100% carnivore diet! One of the best things about the diet was the drastically reduced decision-making, because all I ate was meat, along with water, tea, and coffee. I'm no longer 100% carnivore, but the lesson stuck with me, and I've continued in the spirit of deliberately limiting options, when it means I don't have to think about something as much as I did before.

When I'm not spending time making so many decisions, I get to spend more time saying my affirmations or doing my Coffee Self-Talk, or manifesting my dreams by tapping into beautiful, elevated emotions. Yeah, I'd much rather do that than figure out what shoes to wear.

What about you? Would you benefit from simplifying your life?

How about your meals? Be free to serve a meal that's as simple as... *yogurt!* Or just making a big ol' pile of pancakes. Instead of figuring out a bunch of different side dishes, just serve the one. And look at your whole cooking and eating as a system, and see where you can rinse and repeat on meals.

In Italy, we literally rotate through four different dinners (this was during COVID, so we weren't eating out). All four of the meals were delicious, and four was sufficient for variety, but simple enough to make my shopping and food prep super simple.

Once I became passionate about reducing decisions, it prompted me to take a closer look at other areas of my life. Where else could I simplify? I became re-energized about living a more minimalist lifestyle. I started getting rid of unused items, stuff like knick-knacks and even unused furniture. Guess what I discovered?

First, my whole life felt slightly less cluttered. Like it was easier to think, just because there was less "stuff" around me. And not only that, it was also suddenly much easier to dust and vacuum! *Ha!*

Simplify.

Simplifying means fewer choices, which leaves you with more energy, better decisions, and a better life. So if you enjoy today's fun exercise, and you get a little tingle in your toes as you imagine ways to simplify, that's your soul saying, *yes yes yes!* Listen to it.

Your Turn to Play!

Look around. Do you see anything that could be simplified?

Or look at your calendar. Are there any optional items you've got planned that don't spark joy? Consider canceling, and carving out time for yourself instead.

Have fun with this. Can you simplify cooking? Can you simplify your beauty routine? Your wardrobe? Your household chores? Can you simplify what you carry in your purse? Pro-tip: Carrying a smaller purse does wonders for carrying less. *Simplify.*

You are magnificent!

～

Today's affirmation:

I honor and appreciate myself.

DAY 27: REPEAT, REPEAT, REPEAT

"We're all golden sunflowers inside."

— ALLEN GINSBERG

I don't know about you, but I was never taught in school that the words I say and think could have such a profound effect on my life. I wish they'd told me! I never learned as a child how my thoughts could be creative and magnificent, and that they could help me literally create my destiny.

But I know now, and so does my ten-year-old daughter. She sees and hears me doing my Coffee Self-Talk all the time. She has her own positive self-talk, too.

Today, we're going to take advantage of firing and wiring. The key is repetition. The more you fire thoughts or behaviors, the faster you wire them in your brain. The more times you think amazing things, the more often you feel amazing feelings, and the faster you transform into your dream you.

In the exercise below, you'll expand your morning Coffee Self-Talk and bring it into the rest of your day.

Your Turn to Play!

Choose an uplifting statement from the examples below, or one of your favorite affirmations from your own Coffee Self-Talk script, and then, repeat, repeat, repeat!

Get out your sticky notes. Write down your chosen line of self-talk, or one of your favorite positive affirmations, on six sticky notes.

Here are some examples to choose from:

- I am worthy!
- My needs will always be met!
- I am loved!
- Opportunities are all around me!
- I love life, and life loves me!
- I am magnificent!
- I'm a wonderful, kind person!
- I am patient!
- I am bursting with amazing health!
- I sparkle, shimmer, and shine!

Then get your phone (or to-do list/calendar/notebook/etc.) and add it there, too. The point is having this in multiple places to remind you.

Place your stickies where you'll see them during the day. Every time you see one, stop for ten seconds. Assume a Power Pose, if you like (see Day #14), take a breath, and say your incredibly awesome affirmation out loud, feeling the amazing, related emotions deep down in your bones.

If it's an affirmation for something you aim to be, then imagine how crazy great it would feel if the affirmation were already true. Remember, imagining it *as real* rewires your brain and helps *make it happen*. (If you can't say it out loud, then mouth it.)

You are freakin' talented!

～

Today's affirmation:

I am devoted to me. I am devoted to me. I am devoted to me.

DAY 28: LOVE MANTRA

"Let us dance in the sun, wearing wildflowers in our hair..."

— Susan Polis Schutz

Too often, people don't love themselves enough. They feel silly saying *"I love you"* to themselves, or they don't really feel it. I know, because I felt ridiculous the first time I did it.

Well, that's going to change. Self-love is *where it all starts*. It's the foundation of manifesting your dreams and becoming the "you" that you want to be. No matter what your goal is—weight loss, more energy, more money, more patience—self-love is the first step to getting there. It's the rocket fuel in your rocket.

When you love yourself, you boost your confidence. You feel magical. You experience elevated, happy emotions. When you love yourself, you make better choices for yourself and others. When you love yourself, you love yourself no matter what... mistakes, flaws, and all.

Loving yourself is vital for your magical life! And you're going to love loving yourself. I promise!

Your Turn to Play!

Set a timer for one minute. Take a lovely, deep breath, and in a relaxed state, say, *"I'm Love. I love my life. I love life. I love you, (insert your name)!"* Repeat this until the timer goes off. It doesn't matter if it feels fake or inauthentic. Or weird. As you repeat this, it gets easier and easier. I promise.

Say it again every time you see yourself in the mirror, for the next two weeks. By the end of the first week, the awkwardness will be gone. After the second week, well... just wait and see what happens. A whole new relationship with yourself awaits. (And it may happen much sooner!)

You're worthy of all the love you shower upon yourself!

∾

Today's affirmation:

I'm living a completely new life of self-love, of self-care, and of self-worth. A life of my own design.

DAY 29: MAKE A UNIVERSE BOX

"When we give cheerfully and accept gratefully, everyone is blessed."

— MAYA ANGELOU

A *Universe Box* is a special place for you to send little notes to the universe. Some people call it a "God Box" or a "Life Messages Box." I call mine a Universe Box, but it's actually a red ceramic teapot with a lid. It's cute.

You can choose whatever container you like as your Universe Box.

Of course, you can send messages to the universe with your mind and your heart all day, but the act of physically slipping a note into the Universe Box does something extra. With your Universe Box, you'll write any fears, desires, thoughts of gratitude... anything at all, and put your note into the Universe Box for the universe to handle. Use little scraps of paper or small sticky notes. When you're worried about an issue, or when you desire something, just jot it down as a note and drop it into your Universe Box. Then, the next time the thought comes up, remind yourself that it's in the box, and know that *"The universe has got it!"*

The reason the Universe Box does something more than merely thinking thoughts to the universe is that, when you put the note in the Universe Box, it feels like taking action, and it offers a sense of literally letting go. Surrender. Release. It's like the physical version of how journaling gets things out of your mind, so that you can have a clear and focused head and heart. The Universe Box is similar. By writing your desires on little pieces of paper and letting go of them, it frees up space in your brain.

Your Universe Box can be a shoebox, or a glass mason jar, or a basket with a lid, or a water pitcher, or a piggy bank... anything. You can go out and get a special vessel, something fancy or meaningful, but really, anything that'll hold your notes will do.

I remember the first time I looked inside my Universe Box to see what I had written earlier. It was a tea pot in our apartment in Italy. Due to an unexpected turn of events, we were heading back to the United States. We planned on returning to Italy, but with COVID raging, nothing was certain. I was open to anything.

And so I emptied out my Universe Teapot to see everything that I had put in there over the past six months. It was such an immense joy to read the slips of paper! I had written "pay off debt" two times, "money," "book review stress," and "Fiery Fate" (the working title of one of my romance novels, which I later changed), and more. And I realized how, in the moments I wrote those down, I had been feeling either excitement or tension, and I wanted to just let it go. Which I did by writing on those tiny slips of paper and putting them into my little Universe Teapot.

The amazing thing... the universe *delivered*. None of those are issues anymore. I finished the romance book, reviews no longer affect my mood, our income has increased, and the debt is gone.

You don't ever have to revisit your pieces of paper, but when I did, it was fun. If you like, you can just keep adding notes to your Universe Box, and then one day, dump them all into the trash or recycle, and never look at what you wrote. Or maybe you'll look at them every Sunday. Or once a year, and see how far you've come, or revisit things that you still want to work on.

Your Turn to Shine!

Create your own Universe Box. Then, set aside some small scraps of paper or sticky notes and a pen, so it's always waiting and ready for you. Anytime you feel a desire, or a wish, or a fear, or a lovely thought you want to share with the universe, write it down on a little piece of paper, fold it up, and tuck it into your Universe Box. If you like, you can write the same thing multiple times over multiple days. And if you have a family, consider giving everyone access to the Universe Box so they can place their own orders with the universe.

You are vibrant with rainbow energy.

Today's affirmation:

The truth of my love abounds. My self-love is the foundation of my happiness.

DAY 30: DREAM BIG DAY

"Happiness is the meaning and the purpose of life, the whole aim and end of human existence."

— ARISTOTLE

You are safe to dream big. To think big. To imagine a life so different from what you live now, larger than you could ever have imagined. You have the right.

If you don't like your life, change it.

Nothing is off limits. If there is something big in life you want, you can manifest it. You just train yourself to absorb and put out its unique type of energy, its elevated emotions. And then start taking the steps to make it happen.

I'm not talking about a specific goal you want to attain. Goals are great, but this exercise is different. Goals are necessarily specific... *don't be limited by them!* I'm talking about the *grand story* of your life. Your own personal character arc. The story of who you are, and who you aspire to *BE.* I'm talking about dramatic themes! Focusing on a big dream, or a fundamental change in lifestyle. To the life of your dreams. Instead of merely thinking, for example, *"I want to write a book,"* say to yourself:

"I live the life of a writer."

What would living that life mean? Visualize it, write it down, down to the tiniest details of your day... what you do from the moment you awake, to when you go to sleep. Imagine how living that life would *feeeel,* waking up each morning, and sitting down to write in this epically big, dreamy life. How would you live? Where would you travel? What experiences would you seek to stimulate and inform your creativity?

In December of 2018, I took a bit of a gamble. I decided I wanted to become a millionaire. I put a stake in the ground, even went so far as to write about it on my blog. In one life-changing blog post, I declared my intentions to the world.

To be clear, I was not a millionaire yet.

In fact, I was far from it. *Gulp...*

But I figured that waiting until after it happened to tell the story would be too safe. Kinda lame. Why not share the journey? I mean, there's no shortage of books published by people *after* they become rich, claiming to have the secret formula. But you never hear the stories of the people who tried and failed (this is called *survivorship bias*). I figured it would be much more ballsy to say at the outset, *Hell yeah,* I'm gonna do it... *and then do it.*

Over the next few weeks, I started blogging about my process, and what I started calling the *Happy Sexy Millionaire* lifestyle. It doesn't actually require a million dollars— it's just a fun label for having an abundance mindset. I didn't know *how* specifically I would become a happy sexy millionaire... I had no plan. But I intuitively understood how I should look, think, and feel.

So that's where I started.

I knew I should possess a certain confidence—knowledge that I'm capable of doing this, like it's a foregone conclusion—and show it in the way I walk and talk, with an elevated level of energy every day, and a spectacular sparkle about me. (I often envisioned how Edward, the nice vampire in the *Twilight* series, sparkled in the sunlight.) I knew I would have a sexy and playful gleam in my eye.

I also knew the "millionaire" part meant *freedom*. Freedom meant having options. It meant easy, relaxed shoulders. It meant smiles. And, yes, money. But, again, I didn't yet know *how* the money would manifest. So I focused on the dreamy life, the dreamy thoughts, the dreamy feelings.

I let my subconscious and the universe work out the details, in the background, while I worked on the magical parts, preparing myself to be worthy, ready to receive.

I'm not saying I wouldn't work... I work very hard. I just didn't have a plan yet, and I knew that would come later. You could say I started out by doing prep work, and working "on me."

I thought about the level of comfort that my Happy Sexy Millionaire life would bring me. I thought about the level of security I would feel—physically, financially, and mentally. I imagined the awe I'd feel waking up every day living this dreamy life.

That is how you train yourself to realize the energy and visions in your dreams. By repeating them over and over, until the brain accepts it as 100% true. A done deal. As though you were born for it, and it could be no other way. Like it's your *destiny*.

Imagine the heroic confidence you automatically acquire as any and all self-doubt just melts away. No bravery required! No fear! You simply expect to succeed.

And then, as if by magic... the next steps just appear in front of you.

Your Turn to Play!

Today, spend a few minutes thinking about the big, beautiful, exciting, dreamy life you want. Go ahead and chew on it, sniff it, look at it, inspect it with an open heart and mind, and most importantly.... *feeeel* it.

If you keep a journal, go crazy, fill as many pages as you can, fleshing out the details of this future life of yours.

If you don't journal, consider starting today... what a way to start *with a bang!*

If you don't want to, then just write an email to yourself, as though you were writing to a friend and confidant, describing what you imagine. The point is to write it down. Writing it will draw more details out of you and provide you with a written record to check against in the future.

You don't even have to look at it when you're done. Just tuck it away for now. Committing it to paper is like placing an order with the universe, and your subconscious.

They're both listening.

You are splendid.

≈

Today's affirmation:

My needs are always met. I am capable. I am safe. I am AWESOME!

CONCLUSION & FREE PDF

You now have 30 more nuggets—tools, tricks, and bits of inspiration—to stuff up your sleeves and pull out anytime you need a little extra magic. They are how I bridge the time between my morning Coffee Self-Talk and my night-time Pillow Self-Talk, especially when I need a little boost.

Life isn't meant to be hard, but sometimes we need help navigating its waters. Sometimes, we need a reminder to keep our spirits elevated. When you do it regularly, it not only makes life more enjoyable, it makes life *magical.*

Free PDF

For a free, printable PDF with cut-out affirmations and fun reminders to hang on your refrigerator, email me at:

Kristen@KristenHelmstetter.com

Please specify that you'd like the:

"Daily Reader #2 Fridge Stuff"

∼

I have a HUGE favor to ask of you.

If you would help me, I'd greatly appreciate it. I'd love it if you would leave a review for this *Coffee Self-Talk Daily Reader #2* on Amazon. Reviews are incredibly important for authors, and I'm extremely grateful if you could write one!

∼

Podcast

You can hear me on the *Coffee Self-Talk with Kristen Helmstetter* podcast wherever you listen to podcasts or at:

https://anchor.fm/kristen-helmstetter

And come join our fun and lively group for readers:

Facebook.com/groups/coffeeselftalk

∼

What's Next?

Here are the other books in the Coffee Self-Talk family:

KRISTEN HELMSTETTER

COFFEE SELF-TALK

5 minutes a day to start living your magical life

International Bestseller – Over 100,000 Copies Sold
Coffee Self-Talk: 5 Minutes a Day to Start Living Your Magical Life

Coffee Self-Talk is a powerful, life-changing routine that takes only 5 minutes a day. Coffee Self-Talk transforms your life by boosting your self-esteem, filling you with happiness, and helping you attract the magical life you dream of living. *All this, with your next cup of coffee.*

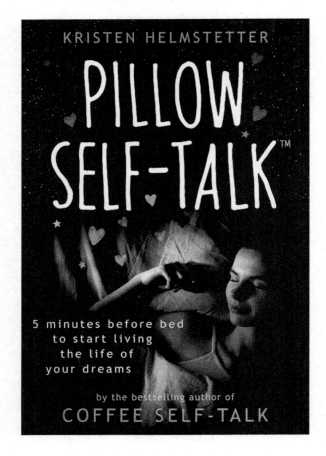

Pillow Self-Talk:
5 Minutes Before Bed to Start Living the Life of Your Dreams

End your day with a powerful nighttime ritual to help you manifest your dreams, reach your goals, find peace, relaxation, and happiness... all while getting the *best sleep ever!*

Wine Self-Talk:
15 Minutes to Relax & Tap Into Your Inner Genius

There is a source of sacred wisdom in you. *Wine Self-Talk* is a simple, delicious ritual to help you relax, unwind, and tap into your inner genius.

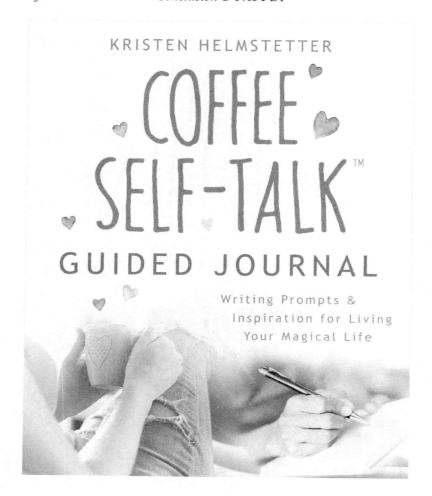

The Coffee Self-Talk Guided Journal:
Writing Prompts & Inspiration for Living Your Magical Life

This guided journal keeps you *lit up and glowing* as you go deeper into your magical Coffee Self-Talk journey. Experience the joy of journaling, mixed with fun exercises, and discover hidden gems about yourself. Get inspired, slash your anxiety, and unleash your amazing, badass self.

The Coffee Self-Talk Blank Journal

This is literally a blank journal (with lines). There are no words, except for a one-page intro.

This blank journal provides a place to write your own scripts, as well as journal your thoughts and progress. You could use any notebook, but readers have asked for a matching journal to make things fun and help reinforce their daily Coffee Self-Talk ritual.

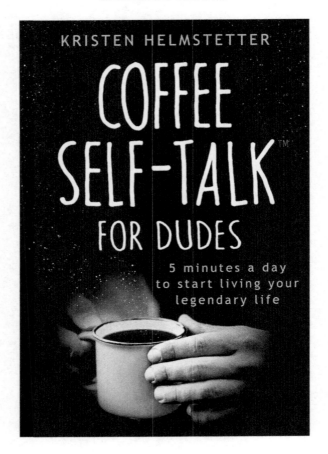

Coffee Self-Talk for Dudes:
5 Minutes a Day to Start Living Your Legendary Life

This is a special edition of *Coffee Self-Talk* that has been edited to be more oriented toward men in the language, examples, and scripts. It is 95% identical to the original *Coffee Self-Talk* book.

Coffee Self-Talk for Teen Girls:
5 Minutes a Day for Confidence, Achievement & Lifelong
Happiness

This is written for girls in high school (ages 13 to 17 years old). It covers the same ideas as *Coffee Self-Talk*, and applies them to the issues that teen girls face, such as school, grades, sports, peer pressure, social media, social anxiety, beauty/body issues, and dating.

Coffee Mugs & More

Visit CoffeeSelfTalk.com for all kinds of fun stuff to add more self-talk to your day:

- Coffee mugs
- Travel mugs
- Water bottles
- Notebooks
- And more

Readers of this book get a 10% discount (one-time use only). Just enter the following at checkout.

Coupon code: **CSTBOOK10%**

Printed in Great Britain
by Amazon